# The authors

John Silvester has been a crime reporter in
Melbourne since 1978. He worked for
*The Sunday Times* 'Insight' team in London
in 1990, and has co-authored several crime
books, including the best-seller *Underbelly*.
He is currently senior crime writer for *The
Age* and an expensive but strangely popular
after-dinner speaker.

Andrew Rule has been a journalist since
1975 and has worked in newspapers,
television and radio. He wrote *Cuckoo*, the
true story of the notorious 'Mr Stinky' case,
and has edited and published several other
books, including the original *Underbelly*.
He is the deputy editor of *The Sunday Age*
and charges much more reasonably for
after-dinner speaking.

Silvester and Rule won the prestigious Ned
Kelly Award for True Crime writing for
*Underbelly 3*.

# UNDERBELLY 11

## More true crime stories

# UNDERBELLY 11

Published in Australia by
Floradale Productions Pty Ltd and Sly Ink Pty Ltd
November 2007

Distributed wholesale by
Gary Allen Pty Ltd,
9 Cooper Street,
Smithfield, NSW
Telephone 02-9725 2933

Cover: Robert Klinkhamer
Typesetting and layout: Nicole Buttner

*Underbelly 11*
*More True Crime Stories*

ISBN – 0 9775440 5 2

❛ The culture in the underworld has changed. We have, for at least the foreseeable future, broken the model that there is honour among thieves ❜

– Paul Coghlan, former
Director of Public Prosecutions,
now Supreme Court Judge

# Contents

# CHAPTER 1

# Jacked off

'He's a monster, you don't know what he's like.'

IN HIS 22 years as a fireman, Brian Thompson had attended many tragic accidents, but there was something about the scene that day – where a young mother was crushed under her own car – that left him with a lasting sense of unease.

At first Thompson was too busy looking for signs of life to worry about the cause of death. But when he couldn't find a pulse and the victim's skin was cold to the touch, he told a neighbour frantically trying to use his own jack to lift the car that it was too late. She was gone.

Anne Louise Crawford, former primary school teacher and mother of two young children, lay dead under her 1983 brown Ford Fairlane. The car had apparently slipped off the jack as she scrambled for a wheel nut under the sedan while trying to change the driver's side front tyre on the morning of May 6, 1988.

The sedan dropped, crushing her skull and killing her instantly – the momentum was so powerful that it flattened the bottom of the metal front disk on impact with the concrete floor. When he realised there was nothing he could do, Thompson glanced around the carport of the neat suburban home in De Havilland Avenue, Strathmore Heights. He saw a stray wheel nut near the sump, a tyre on the ground next to the car and a second leaning against the house. It fitted perfectly the theory that the victim, 35, was changing a tyre when the car slipped.

He also noticed the jack was poorly constructed and covered in what he described as 'oriental writing' – not the standard issue for the Australian-made Ford.

It looked like a straightforward case of a momentary lapse of judgment combined with unimaginable bad luck. That is, until the veteran fireman walked over and felt the two tyres. 'They were both obviously flat,' he would later recall.

Why, he wondered, would someone struggle to change a tyre with a dodgy jack when the spare was also useless? It didn't make sense and quickly became the talk of some of the emergency workers at the scene.

'This was the subject of discussion between myself and other people,' he said.

Another man used to trying to find order in chaos was ambulance officer Greg Sassella, who would rise through the ranks to become chief executive officer of the Metropolitan Ambulance Service.

After the firemen used emergency airbags to gently lift the car to free the body, he immediately saw the crushing injuries that ended Anne Crawford's life.

He escorted the body to the Coroner's Court, where he noticed an unexplained injury. Four small bruises at the back of her left bicep described as 'in the shape of four fingertips'.

It was as if a right-handed attacker had grabbed her roughly by the arm. It could have been a vital clue if police were looking. But they weren't.

A cursory examination of the scene by a trained detective would have raised further suspicions – such as why a woman with a reputation for neatness would choose to change from the tracksuit she wore during her morning walk into freshly laundered camel slacks and white shirt before attempting to change a filthy tyre.

And why, if she was under the car searching for a wheel nut when she was crushed, she was found flat on her back.

Or how the safe Ford-issue jack had mysteriously gone missing and would never be recovered. Or why two photographs in the hallway inside the house had been displaced as if knocked in a struggle.

An expert may have noticed that the victim's perfect set of pinkish-brown false fingernails had been damaged, leaving the right index one missing.

A homicide investigator may have considered that the nail could have been lost while Anne Crawford fought for her life before she was placed unconscious under her own car and then crushed.

The area would have been declared a crime scene and a search would have been ordered to look for evidence, including the missing false fingernail and the Ford jack.

Perhaps the search would have found the pillowcase carelessly tossed on a pile of clothes in the laundry by a killer who used it to cover her face when he bashed her unconscious before he positioned her under the car to make murder look like misadventure.

But there were no detectives called. Local uniform police attended and declared it an accident. From the day of the tragedy the case seemed as dead as the unfortunate victim.

Perhaps they were swayed by the superficial. This was a nice family, living in a nice street in a nice neighbourhood. Best not to pry too deeply and further upset the family and friends of the poor woman who lost her life. There were no pictures taken, no search ordered and no forensic examination undertaken. The car was removed to be sold just weeks later to an air force officer in Canberra and the fire brigade hosed down the concrete carport floor to remove any sign of blood that would disturb and traumatise Anne Crawford's husband and children.

Later, when police decided to take another look, they found the crime scene was hopelessly compromised.

From the beginning, there were many clues that this was no accident.

But it would take police eighteen years to prove it was murder.

THE only witness who could explain to police the events that led to the death of Anne Crawford was her husband, Ron. A chemist with a strange nature, an entrepreneurial flair and a wandering eye, he was building a growing business of retail pharmacies.

According to Crawford, his wife was backing out of their long drive with their two children about 8.10am when he noticed the car was scraping on the ground from a flat tyre.

Anne slowly drove back into the carport and, according to his version of events (which would later change), he opened the boot and removed the spare tyre. He then looked for the jack and found it to be missing.

'I asked Anne where the jack was, and she wasn't able to remember what happened to it.'

He then planned to change the tyre so he grabbed the jack from his Toyota Landcruiser. But realising he was running late for work he decided to return to the job later. They took their young son to school and their daughter to kindergarten in the Toyota.

He dropped Anne home after she bought some milk, kissed

her goodbye and told her, 'I will be home before lunch so just leave everything and I'll fix it'.

Later Crawford's story subtly changed. When he was questioned, rather than just being allowed to tell his story, he wouldn't be able to recall who opened the boot and who removed the spare tyre – avoiding the sticking point of why he did not notice the second tyre was flat and unusable.

In his second version, he claimed his wife declared she wanted to change the tyre, although he insisted he would do it by lunchtime. He said that when she had replaced a wheel two months earlier (implying she lost the Ford issue jack in the process), he had chastised her, stating he felt it was his job.

The subtext was obvious: the dutiful husband was available to fix the problem while the headstrong wife took on a job beyond her capabilities, with tragic consequences.

While stopping short of declaring it was her fault, he made it clear it certainly wasn't his.

When he drove up his street around 11.45 to change the tyre as promised, he saw the fire brigade and ambulance outside his house.

As he approached, Thompson gently placed a hand against his chest and guided him away. No husband should be allowed to see his wife in such a devastating scene.

Crawford would tell sympathetic police they had been happily married for thirteen years and were busy planning for the future with their son, seven, and daughter, four. They had bought a large block and were planning to build their dream home.

It would be nearly a month before police started to think that perhaps Anne Crawford's death was more sinister than first thought.

While some close to the Crawfords had their immediate doubts and the death had become the gossip of the neighbourhood, the reason for the police re-examination came from a seemingly unlikely source.

It was when a notorious armed robber tried to cut a deal by providing police with information on unsolved crimes and began to talk about the death of Anne Crawford.

The armed robber said Ronald William Edward Crawford, successful chemist, devoted family man and now grieving widower, had effectively put his wife's life out for tender and had been trying to find a violent criminal to take the contract for years.

The armed robber would claim he had been offered (and refused) the contract for $25,000.

The new information was passed to Detective Sergeant John Johnstone, an experienced investigator who could smell a rat and was trained to deal with them.

Police investigations would find the middle-class chemist had several unexplained links to the underworld. His connections were intriguing. He was an associate of bandit Frankie Valastro (who was shot dead by police in 1987), the armed robber talking to police, and another violent criminal who can only be identified as PS.

The armed robber told detectives that he'd been shot in 1984 and Crawford had provided him with drugs and arranged medical treatment through a Moonee Ponds doctor who would not report the incident to police.

Crawford was a shooter who kept several firearms at home. The armed robber-turned-informer claimed the chemist provided him with a .38 revolver for a stick-up in 1984.

Johnstone was able to establish that the chemist drove to Bendigo Prison twice to visit PS, signing in using the alias Jonathan Hart from his favourite television show, *Hart to Hart*.

In the series, self-made millionaire Hart and his beautiful wife are amateur detectives who are in constant danger from serious criminals. When asked by Johnstone why he had visited the notorious prisoner, Crawford replied: 'He was lonely.' Prison records show the middle-class chemist visited the career criminal in jail at least four times.

The prisoner told police the chemist had bought him a new pair of runners on each visit. Such acts of generosity seemed out of character for a man who was known to be careful with his money.

PS told police Crawford was well known in the underworld and provided drugs for some of his criminal contacts, but he said he had no knowledge of a murder contract on Anne Crawford.

There was another point that interested Johnstone about the prison visits. The seemingly happily married man turned up at jail with his mistress – or at least one of them.

He would tell Johnstone that while he had multiple affairs, he was happily married. 'He stated that at times he had the best of both worlds,' the investigator said.

Johnstone dug deeper and found Crawford had hired a car from Hertz the day before the death but did not return the car to the Tullamarine depot. It was collected the day after Anne's death from the rooftop car park of the Westfield Shopping Centre in Airport West, where Crawford had a chemist shop.

The keys were in the car and the doors were unlocked – it was another action out of character for Crawford, who was known to be security conscious. It had travelled 301 kilometres.

Much later, police would speculate Crawford drove the car 150 kilometres to Euroa, where he paid PS $10,000 to kill his wife, before returning to the shopping centre.

As part of the investigation, a police expert from the accident investigation squad used a police car and the Toyota jack to reconstruct the death.

He found the jack stiff to use and suggested 'a female could have trouble raising the vehicle sufficiently to clear the wheel for removal'.

He also found the jack, designed for an off-road vehicle with a higher wheelbase, could only be placed under the Ford at a point where it did not fit safely. While it initially remained stable, once Senior Sergeant Robert Le Guier rocked the car sideways, it immediately slipped from the jack.

Certainly, Crawford was deeply disturbed about Johnstone's investigation. So much so that he hid in a friend's house to eavesdrop as the detective interviewed the potential witness. Certainly, at times, he behaved like a man who expected to be charged with murder.

Some of the initial actions of the grief-stricken husband started to take on sinister overtones. Such as why he fought against an autopsy, why he refused to allow family members to view the body and why he demanded a cremation when other members of his family were buried.

Johnstone's 27-page statement, which included a record of interview with Crawford, was a damning document that would have exposed the husband as a womaniser who was suspected of organising his wife's murder.

But it didn't.

Coroner Harley Harber – no doubt concerned that the allegations against Crawford were not corroborated – ordered the court closed when Johnstone gave evidence. Harber made a finding that Anne Crawford died when she was crushed under her car while changing a tyre after she crawled under the vehicle to retrieve a wheel-nut. 'I further find that the deceased contributed to the cause of death.'

Officially Anne Crawford was to blame for her own death – at that stage there was no evidence to suggest otherwise.

Crawford left the court in 1989 with his reputation intact. For the moment.

CRAWFORD was an unhappy child who grew from a painfully shy, hardworking adolescent into a brooding adult driven by the need for financial success.

Born with no pectoral muscles on the left side of his chest and a wasted left arm, he was teased as a child growing up in Pascoe Vale and was self-conscious about his disabilities. 'Kids can be cruel,' he would reflect.

But there was one girl, Anne Bravo, three years his junior at Hadfield High School, who could see beyond his disability. 'Anne and I met at high school. We were high school sweethearts,' he told his Supreme Court murder jury in 2006.

They married on December 28, 1974, and had their first child nearly six years later.

Sexually inexperienced when they married, he would later admit to three affairs during his marriage, but he maintained he was hardworking, loved his wife and children and believed his infidelities would not damage his marriage if Anne remained none the wiser.

But when one girlfriend learnt of another, the results were catastrophic. In November 1985, she rang his wife. Crawford would tell the jury: 'Anne was very, very upset; she was devastated because she had no idea of my relationship with Pauline. She didn't suspect it.'

Perhaps she would have been even more upset if she'd known how he referred to her (according to one of his lovers) as 'horse head' and 'boot face' – never Anne.

The man who was mercilessly teased at school over his disabilities had apparently forgotten the venom of harsh words.

He would later say he and Anne were battling through the tough times and were emerging from the darkness when she died in the accident. He claimed that in her final three days they talked about their problems, staying up late the night before the 'accident'.

When asked by his lawyer: 'Did you resolve your issues?' Crawford responded: 'I thought we did. I thought we covered everything.'

He claimed he agreed to join her in counselling (she was already seeing an expert through the Catholic Church), promised to end his 'friendship' with his lover and began to plan an overseas holiday for that September. In fact, he said, she was to have passport photos taken on the day she died.

Of course the only person who could verify the chemist's claims was his wife – but she had been silenced eighteen years earlier.

There was another version. According to the prosecution, Anne Crawford was on the verge of demanding a divorce – a move that would cripple her husband's expanding chemist business. The prosecution claimed she confided to a friend that her unfaithful husband was 'a bastard' and she intended to leave him.

She would never have the chance.

When one relative urged her to stay in the marriage for the sake of the children she said, 'He's a monster, you don't know what he's like'.

For a man who claimed to be shattered by the death, Ron Crawford made a remarkably quick recovery. Within days of the funeral, he rang the woman he promised his wife he would never see again and asked her to go shopping to buy some clothes for his daughter.

He would not remarry, although he would father a child with another woman.

He would buy a country farm, rent the De Havilland Avenue house and own an Essendon home valued at $1.5 million.

He eventually sold his chemist shops for a total, police estimate, of around $10 million.

On a school reunion internet site, he portrayed himself as

part-mogul and part-martyr, declaring he had 'entered the world of retail pharmacy at Ravech Pharmacy in North Coburg, then expanded the retail "vision" with sites in Airport West, Wantirna, Vermont South, Reservoir, in between raised my children after Anne's tragic death. Now still working five days and two days on the farm'.

The boy who had been teased at school seemed to be saying that he had beaten the odds.

Aged in his 50s, he was able to afford the dream of many middle-aged men – a high-performance imported car with personalised plates. He chose RC-88: his initials, curiously added to the year of his wife's death.

Some detectives suspect the letters were a dark, phonetic private joke about him getting away with murder – Arsey 88.

But while Crawford was getting on with his life, a woman connected with the underworld knew the true story and was quietly stewing.

She knew it was no accident because she also knew it was her ex-husband who all those years ago had accepted the contract to kill.

In 2003, fifteen years after Anne Crawford's death, when it seemed destined to remain the perfect murder, she made a call to the homicide squad. Eventually the information was handed to the specialist cold case crew and finally murder investigators began to examine the case.

The cold case crew of the Melbourne homicide squad (since disbanded in a police reshuffle) was used to spending years reconstructing murder investigations.

Using new methods, such as DNA testing, on old crimes, the detectives' aim was to time warp buried cases into modern investigations.

But when Detective Sergeant Mark Colbert and Senior Detectives David Butler and Wayne Newman were assigned the case, they must have thought it was destined to remain a mystery.

What they had was the ex-wife of a career criminal declaring her ex-husband had been contracted to kill Anne Crawford.

But what they didn't have was a body, as the victim had been cremated, nor did they have forensics from the scene, as the area was never treated as a crime scene, or even officially a murder, as a coroner had declared her death accidental.

They knew that if Ron Crawford had organised the murder, he was unlikely to confess. But they also knew that allies drift apart, friends grow distant and discarded lovers can become ferocious enemies.

They approached one of his old girlfriends, who opened up, saying, 'He's gotten away with it for too long. Anne didn't deserve it ... I know that Ron Crawford did it'.

She had worked in one of his pharmacies from 1979 to 1985 and at first she'd found him cold and rude.

The female staff members called the tall and cold chemist 'Lurch' after the near-silent butler in the 1960s *Addams Family* television series.

But despite her initial judgment, she started to see a softer side in him. When she was sick in 1982, he sent her flowers and they soon became lovers.

She told police that over the next three years, he spoke constantly of getting rid of his wife. She said he estimated it would cost $5000 to have her killed or $10,000 to make sure her body was never found.

She gave sworn evidence that he told her of several plans he had considered, such as rewiring the toaster so she would be electrocuted, dropping the hairdryer in her bath, having her run over by a truck or tossing her from a balcony of an apartment building in Queensland.

When she suggested the less radical approach of a simple

divorce, she claimed he responded that he'd 'worked too hard to lose anything'.

'Why should she get half of his money when he's worked so hard and why should she get the kids?' the ex-lover described Crawford's rhetorical question.

In January 1985, he took out an MLC life insurance policy to update the $20,000 they had taken out two months after they married. With interest, he received $79,029 when she died.

His half-baked plans could have appeared to be the rantings of an angry man and not the thoughts of a ruthless one.

After all, the hair-brained murder schemes appeared to have all been borrowed from B-grade Hollywood thrillers.

But Anne Crawford didn't die in any of the ways her husband discussed – she died in what would appear to have been a one-in-a-million accident.

But in Strathmore lightning does appear to strike twice. Eleven months to the day before Anne Crawford died, a young man, aged just twenty, was killed when the car he was working under slipped off a ramp in the carport of his home.

It was in Boeing Street, which joins De Havilland Avenue about 200 metres from the Crawford home.

It had been the talk of the area, particularly since Anne's best friend lived opposite the house.

It was an obvious and graphic warning to locals to remain rigidly safety conscious when working under cars.

But, according to police, it was more than that. They claim that for Crawford, it was a light bulb moment – the beginning of a plan that almost worked.

FOR the cold case crew, the former girlfriend's recollections may have been graphic but they were uncorroborated. In the eyes of the law, Crawford was still the grieving widower.

So rather than rely on hard evidence, they slowly began to

build the pressure on the main players, hoping the targets would implicate themselves by their present actions to a crime committed fifteen years earlier.

While at first they gathered information and slivers of evidence in secret, by 2004 they were ready to run an open campaign. They began to contact friends and relatives of Crawford, making it clear they were reinvestigating his wife's death.

It was a case of firing a shot just to see which way the rabbits would run.

Police spoke to PS's father, saying they wanted to speak to his son about an old case but stop short of providing any details. The father rang the suspected contract killer to say detectives were looking for him and within 25 minutes PS rang Crawford to talk.

He obviously had no doubts about which case was important enough to reopen so many years later.

As the pressure built, Crawford spoke to confidantes, declaring he didn't want to be subjected to another investigation.

But why would a man who believed his wife died accidentally, be worried about a new investigation and why didn't he wonder why police thought there was a link to PS and the death?

A go-between rang PS to tell him that Crawford intended to refuse to answer police questions when he was interviewed. The message was clear to the career criminal. Everyone should remain silent and the investigation would probably die.

But PS was not the same man who coolly took a contract to kill a woman he didn't know. He had become a police protected witness who had given evidence against some of the most vicious criminals in the state as part of the Walsh Street trial where four men were charged and acquitted over the 1988 murders of police constables Steven Tynan and Damian Eyre.

He had been given a new name and a new life, declaring he was finished with crime.

Now he knew that if he was charged and convicted of the murder, he faced a life in prison and Crawford could walk.

He decided, not for the first time, to get in first.

Just ten weeks into the pressure cooker phase of the operation, PS was interviewed by detectives and admitted he killed Anne Crawford for $10,000 in cash.

He claimed to police that when he walked up the drive, Crawford had already left the car jacked up, with the front tyre removed as arranged.

(Police allege Crawford deflated the second tyre to make sure the vehicle couldn't be fixed before the hit man arrived.)

He rang the front door bell and when Anne answered he grabbed her by the left arm (leaving the four bruises) and forced her back to the lounge room.

He said he placed a pillowcase over her head, punched her in the jaw, knocking her unconscious. He then carried her to the car, placed her under the chassis and just pushed the side of the car so the jack would slip out – exactly as the police reconstruction in 1988 showed.

According to the prosecution, PS rang Crawford from a phone box with the coded message that the murder was complete, saying he couldn't catch up that day because his car was 'stuffed'.

PS pleaded guilty to the murder and was sentenced to a minimum of twelve years jail. It was a light sentence for such a cold-blooded hit but he received a discount because he pleaded guilty and agreed to testify against Crawford.

According to one of Crawford's former girlfriends, when he was considering killing his wife he bragged that his friends inside the police force would protect him.

He told one of his girlfriends, 'I could do it and get away with it. I've got plenty of copper mates who would help me out and cover it up.' His relationship with 'copper mates' resulted in his first trial being aborted on August 23, 2006 as a result of a former policeman friend approaching a member of the jury the previous night in a suburban pub.

The former policeman, an ex-boxer, had been in court watching the case and supporting his mate. He left the police force in 1988 – a few months after Anne's death.

For a man trained in court proceedings to approach a juror was – at the very least – an act of breathtaking stupidity. The approach was made just as PS was being cross-examined by Crawford's lawyers. It was a crucial time in the trial.

The former policeman had always maintained Crawford was innocent. What the jury would have concluded we will never know because Justice Tim Smith had no choice but to abort the trial and immediately set up a new hearing.

A second trial was also aborted and a third was needed. In an unusual move Crawford, 55, chose to give evidence before the jury.

Usually an accused in a murder trial will remain silent as the onus is on the prosecution to prove its case. Put your client in the witness box and you open him up to cross-examination and you lose control of your defence. The move to put the chemist in the witness box smacked of desperation – as if the defence could hear the cell-door closing behind their man.

The widower told the jury he no longer believed his wife was the victim of a horrible accident. Faced with the evidence he now accepted it was murder but he swore he had nothing to do with the crime.

Crawford may have been unfaithful, he may have been callous and he may have been a liar but the defence stressed that did not prove he was the killer.

Crawford's heavyweight barrister, Con Heliotis QC, argued

that PS must have gone to Crawford's home to commit a burglary expecting the house to be empty.

Mr Heliotis, perhaps wisely, did not address the puzzling question of why an experienced criminal would believe a house was empty when there was a car with a flat tyre sitting in the drive.

The defence theory was that when he was Anne Crawford he killed his victim and then made it look like an accident.

No, Crawford was not a killer – he was a victim. His wife was killed and now, so many years later, he was accused of a crime he did not commit.

Court observers say Heliotis's closing address to the jury was masterful and persuasive. It had to be – as some close to the defence thought they were sunk.

Justice Smith dutifully warned the jury to be wary of the uncorroborated testimony of co-accused offenders. PS was a career criminal with a history of dishonesty and violence. By implicating Crawford and pleading guilty, he received a sentence discount. The self-confessed killer was not motivated by conscience but by self-interest.

In contrast Crawford was a middle class family man who had brought up his two children after their mother's death. Even some (but not all) of Anne's family were behind Ron Crawford, refusing to believe he was involved.

In late September, after deliberating for four days, the jury of eight men and four women acquitted Crawford. He left court a free and clearly relieved man. Many were surprised by the verdict and at times his legal team seemed resigned to a guilty verdict. One legal expert present at the trial told the prosecution team, 'You were robbed'.

PS returned to prison to serve his sentence. He deserves no sympathy. He killed a woman he did not know for personal gain.

But the intriguing question is why would a career criminal who knows the system confess after so many years of remaining silent? There was no forensic evidence, no body and no eye-witnesses.

He was convicted purely on the basis of his own confession and he did not make it to clear his conscience.

Police say he did a deal because he was frightened Crawford would get in first and make a statement. But if the chemist was not involved then PS was in the clear – so why talk?

There is no doubt the hit man is guilty, but is he the only one?

# CHAPTER 2

# The face of evil

'He didn't scream, cry or really show any sort of emotion that you would expect from someone with a knife in their leg.'

THE young sailor slumped on the small bed was crying with self-pity when he looked up to see an old school friend walk into the tiny watch-house cell.

It was the first face he had recognised since his arrest two days earlier at the Cerberus Naval Base for the murder of a twelve-year-old girl abducted from a nearby beach.

But what the sailor didn't know was that the 'friend' was not there because of concern for him. In fact, he was a young policeman sent by the homicide squad to persuade the prisoner to talk about past crimes.

The sailor was Derek Ernest Percy. He had been arrested trying to wash away his guilt in the laundry of the naval base just hours after Yvonne Elizabeth Tuohy was grabbed at Ski Beach, Warneet, and then molested, tortured and murdered.

When Percy grabbed Yvonne on the beach he also tried to abduct her twelve-year-old friend, Shane Spiller, who escaped only by threatening him with a tomahawk and then running away.

The nature of the abduction and the manner of the little girl's death led detectives, including elite investigator Dick Knight (later an assistant commissioner) to conclude that this was not Percy's first attack.

It was the 1960s and Australia was reeling from a series of child abductions and murders in four state and territories. The headlines and community fears scarred a generation of baby boomers who later would lock their doors and refuse to let their own children (and later their grandchildren) walk to school or play in parks unsupervised.

The murders of fifteen-year-olds Christine Sharrock and Marianne Schmidt on Sydney's Wanda Beach in January 1965; the disappearance of the three Beaumont children – Jane, aged nine, Arnna, seven, and Grant, four, in Adelaide in 1966; the murder of Allen Redston, a six-year-old grabbed in Canberra in September 1966; Simon Brook, three, killed in Sydney in 1968; and Linda Stilwell, seven, abducted from St Kilda in August 1968. All remain unsolved. For nearly 40 years police have suspected that Percy is the man responsible. Now, after a complex investigation involving old memories and new techniques, they have built a compelling case against Australia's longest-serving prisoner – a man who retreats into his own murky world when confronted with his past.

But back in July 1969, in the cold Russell Street cell the novice policeman, aged just twenty, was supposed to listen to his old schoolmate in the hope he would open up if given a familiar shoulder to cry on.

And it almost worked.

The policeman, who resigned in 1989, has returned to country Victoria for a quieter life and tries not to dwell on the past. But when contacted by cold case unit detectives he immediately knew why they had come calling. Without prompting, he recalled his last conversation with Percy.

'He looked up at me and it appeared that he had been sobbing and was very distraught.'

'He said, "Looks like I've fucked up this time." I said, "It certainly looks like it, Derek".

'Derek put his head in his hands for a while, then he looked up at me again and he had tears in his eyes and panic written all over his face. He also looked at me with a plea for help.'

The schoolmate gently suggested Percy needed psychiatric help and then asked: 'Were there any others, mate?

'Derek put his head in his hands and began to sob again. He said, "I cannot remember".'

The constable, who had never interviewed a murder suspect, encouraged Percy to think, telling him that if he could recall past crimes it could help decide his mental state – implying it might assist him later to plead insanity.

Again Percy cried and said he couldn't remember. This was the same response he had given two days earlier to homicide detectives over the Tuohy murder, until confronted with incontrovertible evidence.

The schoolmate, who had been a policeman for only six months, began the push. 'Well, look, Derek, I'll ask you about some of the ones that I know about. You don't have to say anything. If you remember I will jot it down and it could be used in court. I will try and get it heard all at the same time.'

Asked about Linda Stilwell, Percy again said his memory was blank but then, according to the young policeman, volunteered: 'Yes, I drove through St Kilda that day. I had been at Cerberus in the afternoon and was driving along the Esplanade on the way to the White Ensign Club for some drinks.'

Asked directly if he killed her he said: 'Possibly, I don't remember a thing about it.'

Questioned on Simon Brook, he admitted he was in Sydney at the time and said he had driven his brother to work, turning

**21**

off at the railway cutting where the body was found and returning along the same route.

'I came back home that way.'

The inexperienced policeman, who cannot be named because of a court suppression order, began to pursue his suspect. 'So you drove past the same spot in Sydney on the day Simon Brook was killed?'

Percy said: 'Yes.'

Question: 'Do you remember if you killed him?'

Percy: 'I wish I could. I might have. I just don't remember.'

Question: 'What do you know about the Beaumont children in South Australia?'

Percy: 'I was in Adelaide at the time.'

Question: 'You were what? You remember being in Adelaide when they went missing?'

Percy: 'Yes.'

Question: 'Whereabouts were you, when they disappeared?'

Percy: 'Near the beach. But nothing else.'

They were making startling progress with the suspect placing himself at the crime scenes. Perhaps with more time and pressure Percy would have confessed, as he had done over the Tuohy murder.

But at that moment, the watch-house keeper, a more senior policeman who was perhaps more concerned at protocol than progress, told the junior constable he had no business being in the cell. In order to justify his presence, the young copper had to tell him he was there on an official homicide squad investigation.

The spell was broken. Percy knew his former schoolmate was no longer a friend. He was just another outsider trying to find the secrets of his dark past.

In April 1970 Percy was found not guilty of the murder of Yvonne Tuohy on the grounds of insanity. He has never been convicted of murder but prison officers, psychiatrists, judges, police and welfare officers who have to deal with him consider him the most dangerous man in Australia.

But how reliable are the memories of the policeman, now retired and recalling events of many years ago?

Another school friend, who was called to Russell Street Police Headquarters to make a statement to the homicide squad, saw the young man return from Percy's cell.

'He was visibly upset and shaking. (He) then said, "That fucking bastard, I hope they hang him".' He hasn't changed his mind in almost 40 years.

FOR the cold case unit, the disappearance of Linda Stilwell from St Kilda 36 years earlier was to be a case of tidying up loose ends. It was to be a quick review to provide the coroner with a summary of facts so an inquest could finally be held.

With no realistic chance of finding a body, the unit did not want to be tied up for long when there were other cases seen as more solvable.

But when Senior Detective Wayne Newman started to delve into the disappearance in January 2004 he began to discover evidence, solid and circumstantial, that pointed towards Percy as the hot suspect.

To build a convincing case he would have to show that Percy had an overwhelming propensity to commit crimes in such a unique way, that they were as identifiable as a signature. And to prove that, he would have to examine all the murders and disappearances that police had loosely linked to Percy in the 1960s.

For Newman the quick investigation turned into a two-year journey that connected Percy to many of the baffling murders that had appeared destined to remain unsolved.

It would involve police from four forces, supported by psychiatrists and forensic experts. The investigators, many of whom who were not born when the murders were committed, combined together in a unique operation, codenamed Heats.

First, there were several obvious similarities in the cases. The nine victims were all children. They were taken from public places, and were often last seen near beaches and close to yachts. Experts say child stalkers usually try to find an isolated individual to attack but in the 1960s the killer twice took more than one victim and in another case tried to take a second child.

The same experts say sex killers usually have a crime history. They begin with smaller offences, ultimately building to murder. Yet Percy had no police record before he was arrested for the Tuohy murder.

To establish that Percy had killed more than once, Newman would have to prove the suspect was a serial offender and to do that he would have to examine the quiet country boy who became the monster.

ERNEST Percy had been a NSW railway electrician for nearly 25 years, but with no opportunity for career advancement he took a job with the expanding State Electricity Commission in Victoria, first moving to Chelsea and then relocating his young family to Warrnambool in 1957.

It was a perfect fit. Ernest Percy's passion was sailing and he was a top-level dinghy yachtsman. His eldest son Derek, just nine when they moved to Warrnambool, shared his father's hobby and helped build their Moth class yachts and small catamarans.

Later, the quiet and intense Derek was drawn to the sea and beaches – eventually joining the navy. Even after his arrest he would begin building model boats inside bottles to while away thousands of hours in his prison cell.

In 1961 Ernie Percy was promoted and left Warrnambool for Mount Beauty, near Bright. While the job was more lucrative, sailing opportunities were limited. As compensation the Percys spent their holidays in their caravan, often travelling interstate to yachting competitions in their powerful V8 Studebaker Lark.

Much later police would track these holidays against their murder map from the 1960s with intriguing results.

On February 7, 1961, Derek Percy walked into the small Mount Beauty High School wearing his new uniform – grey shorts, woollen v-neck pullover with green and gold trim, grey shirt and a green and gold striped tie.

He soon became friends with the son of a local tobacco farmer who had also just moved to the town.

This newcomer was one of only a handful of students from the school who liked Percy. Some found him intense, abrupt and at times unsettling. But most found him to be one of those kids who seemed to melt into the background. No-one thought he was dangerous – at least not back then.

When police from Operation Heats approached the high school friend he was 55 and had long since left Mount Beauty to forge a successful career as an engineer. He told them: 'One thing that stood out about Derek was that he was very intelligent. Most or nearly all of us at school had to work and study very hard but not Derek. Derek just seemed to float along and get excellent grades. Who knows what he could have achieved if he'd applied himself.'

He said that when the teenage boys went to talk to the local girls Percy would always hang back. 'I got the impression that Derek was shy, quite shy around girls. I never knew Derek to have a girlfriend.'

Percy was fit, quick and strong enough to play cricket as an accomplished middle-order batsman and to excel at table tennis, but his parents refused to let him play football – fearing he would be injured.

In a rare display of disobedience Percy would sometimes

borrow a friend's gear for the occasional game, persuading his mate's mother to wash the clothes so he would not be caught.

If the Percys were over-protective it was understandable. Their third-born, Brett, died from diphtheria when aged only ten months. They were to have three surviving sons.

Back then many of the students at the school saw Percy as intensely private and content with his small circle of friends. Many noticed his tie was a rough hessian design and not a perfect match for the school pattern – although it was considered close enough to pass. But while sometimes shabbily dressed he did have an object that stood out in the small community. He had a freewheeling red bike with racing 'ram's horn' handlebars. The usually passive boy wrote to the school magazine to ask for a shelter to be built to protect students' bicycles, signing under the name 'Rusty Bike'.

As a boy Derek Percy carried his sharp knife 'everywhere' but in country Victoria that did not make him unusual. In the 1960s a pocketknife was more a tool than a weapon, used to solve a problem rather than create one.

But when Percy used his to help a mate make running repairs to the sole of a shoe during a handball game, there was a glimpse into his future. 'I remember Derek getting his pocketknife out and telling me that he would cut the sole off. I put my foot on Derek's left thigh in similar fashion to when a blacksmith shoes a horse. Derek began to cut the sole off my shoe and all of a sudden the blade went into Derek's left thigh about three-quarters of an inch (about 2cms). The blade went deeply into his thigh and I recoiled back in surprise. I was amazed that Derek just looked fascinated with what had happened. He didn't scream, cry or really show any sort of emotion that you would expect from someone with a knife in their leg.

'I thought his reaction was extremely odd,' the friend said. 'He seemed happy about it.'

KIEWA Valley's hydro-electric scheme was nowhere near as grand as the Snowy Mountains scheme, but in post-war Victoria it gave hard-working tradesmen the chance to live in an area long considered one of the prettiest in the state.

So much so that when a small town was built in 1949 to house the workers at the foot of Mount Bogong it was simply named Mount Beauty.

With a population of less than 2000 and access to some of Victoria's best ski fields and trout streams it was considered an ideal spot to raise a family.

It was so peaceful that hundreds of police and their families regularly holidayed there – the Police Association providing a house to help members with cheap accommodation.

There was little violent crime, virtually no nightlife and no need to lock houses or cars.

But in late 1964 a small crime wave began. More annoying than threatening it soon became the subject of local gossip – and the whispering nominated the young Percy boy as the likely suspect.

In 1964, clothes – particularly women's underwear – began to disappear from washing lines around the town. Until around this time Percy had been a model student and teachers appointed him a school prefect for 1965. They couldn't understand why in that year the bright boy's marks plummeted. They didn't know then that he was beginning a losing struggle with his inner demons.

As the locals began to suspect Percy was the mystery thief the word spread around the cricket club that Ernie Percy threatened to sack any hydro worker who suggested his son was the snowdropper. But by late 1964 at least two locals knew that Derek Percy was the culprit and that he was much worse than just a petty thief. He was dangerously disturbed and, they believed, a potential killer.

On a warm Sunday afternoon two teenagers, Kim White and Bill Hutton, walked about five kilometres out of town to the local swimming hole known as the Gorge. From their vantage point above the West Kiewa River they saw what they thought was a girl in a petticoat. They crept closer, hoping they had stumbled on someone skinny-dipping, when they realised it was Percy in a pink negligee.

Hutton disliked Percy, recalling he had a habit of repeatedly spitting and seemed to enjoy hitting fellow students with his leather and metal key chain. 'I can remember that Derek was very good at whipping the other kids and used to take great delight in inflicting pain on others.'

Now from their moral and physical high ground they had their chance to get some dirt on the strange kid at school. At first Hutton picked up a rock ready to throw near Percy to startle and humiliate him but White suggested they should sit quietly and watch.

With typical laconic country humour, White's comment on seeing a schoolmate in a negligee was, 'Well, at least it fits'.

But any humour evaporated when Percy began to slash wildly at the clothing, then cut and stabbed at the crotch of a pair of female underpants. From Hutton's vantage point he could see Percy's face. 'I would describe Derek's eyes as being full of excitement, a glazed look, but I recall there was something very cold and sinister in the look,' he told police from Operation Heats.

Percy then dressed and left. The shaken pair went to the river's edge looking for a body because they believed they had looked into the eyes of a killer.

So disturbed were the boys they reported the incident to a senior teacher at the school the next day. So bizarre were their claims the teacher lectured them on the dangers of making up stories. White remembers the teacher warned him: 'Don't go bringing those sorts of things up, it'll only cause you trouble.' Both Hutton and White confronted Percy, who denied what they had seen. Most of the students thought the two had fabricated the story.

After all, Percy was the obedient student seen as prefect material, while his accusers were knockabout teenagers who loved a little mischief. Five years later, when Percy was arrested for the Tuohy murder, several old classmates rang to apologise.

It was not the only time that clear signs of Percy needing psychiatric help were ignored.

The following year Ernie Percy took a job with the Snowy Mountains Scheme and moved his family across the border to Khancoban in NSW. But Derek stayed and boarded with a family in Mount Beauty to allow him to finish school.

The woman who lived next door remembers how the new boarder would sit outside with his red bike upturned watching the wheels spin. She said that while hanging out the washing she could feel the teenager watching her.

Now in her 70s, she says that one Saturday she took her two daughters, then aged seven and nine, out to visit a relative. She locked the house, putting the key in a tin outside the door.

When they returned they found the girls' wardrobes had been rifled and their underwear and dresses stolen.

The mother reported the theft of the twenty dresses to the local police sergeant who asked her if she suspected anyone. 'I told him that I did suspect someone but I didn't want to name him. The person I suspected was Derek Percy.'

A few weeks later a local found some of the dresses in a bundle hidden under some blackberry bushes. But it was what was found with the clothing that made the discovery particularly disturbing.

There was a girl doll, with the eyes marked as if blinded, and newspaper clippings of women in bikinis. In each case the eyes were pencilled out and the bodies mutilated with razor blades discovered with the package. The slashes would match some of the wounds inflicted on the children murdered around Australia in the 1960s.

The blinded doll belonged to the girl next door to where Percy was living.

Percy finally moved from Mount Beauty to join his family in Khancoban after he failed his leaving certificate (Year 11) exams in 1965 – a disappointing result for a student with an IQ of 122 and deemed to be of 'superior intellect'.

In his entry in the Mount Beauty school magazine the secretive Percy revealed a little of his concealed thoughts.

His favourite saying was: 'It depends'. Perpetual occupation: 'Isolating myself'. Ambition: 'Playboy'. Probable fate: 'Bachelor'. Pet aversion: 'Girls'.

When Percy left the town the incidents of snowdropping stopped – only to begin near his new home in Khancoban. There were also reports of a peeping Tom in the town. One local woman said she had seen someone in a school uniform running away from her house.

Percy repeated his leaving certificate at Corryong High School. He seemed shy to the point of reclusive. He was now in the same class as his younger brother, who was a popular boy. The younger Percy 'distanced myself' from Derek and they did not socialise at school.

But Derek and his brother did form a small band, the Rising Sons, with the elder one on lead guitar. The band shocked their small local following when Derek Percy took to the stage dressed in a frock, years ahead of the androgynous glitter rock of the next decade. Meanwhile, a neighbour found that Percy had lured her six-year-old daughter into the family caravan to sexually assault her.

When the girl's father found out he decided to deal directly with Ernie Percy rather than call police.

'Ernie took the matter seriously and was obviously concerned about what I was telling him,' the parent was to recall. 'Ernie gave me an undertaking that this would not happen again.'

And it didn't. At least not in Khancoban.

It is now clear that while both parents said they thought their eldest son was shy, bright and normal, deep down they had growing fears about his tendencies.

One Mount Beauty local said that while Mrs Percy allowed her middle son freedom to wander the district, big brother Derek was kept on a much tighter rein.

'Derek had to get permission to go anywhere with us outside of school hours and she would question his intentions,' he recalled.

Ernie Percy would later tell NSW police he had once found the troubled boy dressed in women's clothing. It appears he kept the incident a secret – perhaps hoping it was just a phase.

The parents also found some disturbing sexual writings from their son and immediately burnt them.

Later, Percy's grandmother found letters filled with thoughts she would only describe as 'rude'. Percy denied they were his, saying they had been written by another boy. Again they were burnt.

'Both Ernie and myself dismissed the matter and nothing more was done,' his mother later said. But Percy began writing of his bizarre and violent sexual fantasies in 1965 – around the time his school marks collapsed.

He continued the self-incriminating habit for years. Much later police would allege the writings were plans for the crimes he was to commit and directly linked him to the series of unsolved child murders.

At the end of 1966, having finally completed his leaving certificate, Percy was ready to leave Corryong High.

Ernest Percy also decided to leave the mountains and move into private enterprise. He invested his payout in a Shell service station in Newcastle.

Derek tried matriculation (Year 12) in a NSW school, dropped out, worked at the service station, then in November 1967, joined the navy, graduating the following February at the top of his class.

Nearly four decades after that, detectives from Operation Heats began the massive task of trying to piece together his movements around Australia over the crucial four-year period of the 1960s.

They knew the Percys often took their caravan to holiday near beaches during yachting regattas. They also could prove Percy was harbouring thoughts of molesting and killing children at the same time as the series of shocking abductions were carried out in four states and territories.

But was it simply a series of coincidences? How could a bright teenager living in country Victoria grab children hundreds of kilometres away? And how could a young sailor murder and return to his base undetected?

To begin, police had to go back to the start. They headed to the archives to review the files of missing and murdered children. Detectives turned into historians as they tracked down details of events that began when Sir Robert Menzies was still Prime Minister. Some witnesses were dead and exhibits had been destroyed. It was never going to be easy.

At first they expected to find information that would discount Percy but the further they looked the stronger the link became.

ON a windy Monday – January 11, 1965 – teenage neighbours Marianne Schmidt and Christine Sharrock left Brush Road to catch a train at the nearby West Ryde railway station to Sydney's popular Cronulla Beach area.

The two girls took Marianne's four younger brothers and sisters with them for the day out. They arrived at the beach about 11am and set up a picnic. Later they went for a walk but the younger children began to complain about the wind whipping up the sand, stinging their legs.

The fifteen-year-old girls decided to push on, sending the youngsters back to a sheltered area near Wanda Beach.

When Peter Schmidt, ten, saw his sister and her friend heading in the wrong direction to pick up their possessions, he yelled out to them but they kept walking away. He then noticed they were with a blond teenage boy. His brother, Wolfgang, seven, said he saw them talking to the teenager earlier and heard him ask their names. He also said the youth had a knife in a scabbard and carried a spear.

The girls' mutilated bodies were found next day partially buried behind a sand dune.

There were several obvious similarities between the Yvonne Tuohy case and the Wanda beach killings.

In both cases, the victims were taken from the beach and dumped nearby. In Wanda Beach the offender took two victims and in the Melbourne case Percy tried to abduct two but Shane Spiller had escaped from him. (Spiller never recovered from the trauma and disappeared in unexplained circumstances in 2002.) In both cases the killer asked his victims their names before abducting them.

The crotch area of one of the Wanda Beach girls' bathers had been cut. Percy was seen slashing female underwear at Mount Beauty in late 1964 – just weeks earlier.

However, that was in Victoria – not in Sydney.

But witnesses told police they remember the Percys went to Sydney that year for their summer break. The mother of one of Percy's closest friends in Mount Beauty told detectives: 'I can recall reading about the murders of young girls at Wanda

Beach, Sydney. I can remember saying to my son Peter that Derek was in Sydney at the time of the murders. Peter told me not to be silly. I have always felt that Derek may be a suspect in that case.'

Ernie Percy, a champion Moth class sailer, tried to arrange his holidays to coincide with yacht races around Australia. During December 1964 and January 1965 a national yachting regatta was held at the Botany Bay Yachting Club – the Australian Moth Class Championship. The club was a short distance from Wanda Beach.

At the time Percy's grandparents lived in Ryde, just 1.7 kilometres from the West Ryde Railway station where the two girls caught the train on the day they were murdered.

The police theory is that Percy saw the girls with the younger children at the station and followed them to the beach, where he struck up a conversation.

When Percy abducted Tuohy he had a knife in a scabbard tied to his waist in the same manner as the blond teenage suspect at Wanda Beach.

Victorian police inspector Tim Attrill was a young sailor who served with Percy on the training ship HMAS *Queensborough*. He says Percy was a cold person, that he loved small yachts and seemed to be able to disappear when off duty.

Sailors would carry knives on a leather 'gun belt' when carrying out duties such as cutting ropes. But Attrill remembers that Percy kept his strapped to his side at all times – even when there was no need. 'He seemed to love it.'

After police arrested Percy at Cerberus they found a green-covered diary with Percy's hand-written notes, describing in detail his urges to sexually abuse, torture, murder and mutilate children.

They also found drawings of naked children and adult women along with pictures of nude women at the beach.

In one excerpt Percy wrote he would force one of his victims to drink beer. Autopsy results showed that Christine Sharrock had a blood alcohol reading equivalent to drinking about 300mls of beer.

In his murder blueprint he wrote about abducting and killing 'two girls at Barnsley' – a beach in northern NSW. Police claim it was a simple code for Wanda Beach.

Years later jail authorities seized more writings that included coded references to the graphic sexual assault and murder of children. It shows that Percy used codes to conceal his actions and thoughts.

Back in 1965 some in the Mount Beauty area saw the resemblance to Percy – who at the time had light-coloured hair – in the photofit issued of the blond suspect. But it would be more than a year before someone would raise it with Percy himself.

It was 1966 and Percy had moved to Corryong High when classmate Wayne Gordes decided to tease the new student after he saw the obvious resemblance to the photofit. 'I jokingly thought to myself, "That's Derek", because of the description and I knew that they went to a beach in Sydney.

'A group of us were standing in the quadrangle when Derek Percy walked past. I said, "We know it was you that killed those girls in Sydney. You have the same haircut and we know you were there."

'With that Derek went berserk. He said, "Don't you say that." Derek was at the stage where I think he wanted to fight me for what I had said. I had never seen Derek behave like that before and it was quite out of character. I thought to myself, "Relax, Derek, it's just a joke". Derek then walked off.'

ON Wednesday January 26, 1966 the Beaumont children, nine-year-old Jane, seven-year-old Arnna, and four-year-old Grant, caught the bus from their Somerton Park home to Glenelg Beach. They left about 9.45am for the five-minute trip. Their mother, Nancy, expected them home about midday.

They were spotted on the bus and a friend of Jane's later saw them sitting on the lawn of the Holdfast Bay Sailing Club about 11am. Later, a man was seen talking to them and at 11.45 the children bought a pie and two pasties from Wenzel's Bakery in Jetty Road.

Almost certainly the man gave them cash for the food as the children paid with a one-pound note – more money than their mother had given them. They were never seen again.

The description of the suspect was a man in his 30s with light brown short swept-back hair parted on the left side, a thin face and clean-shaven. He had a suntanned complexion and was wearing blue bathers with a white stripe down the side.

So could it have been Percy? He was only seventeen at the time but was sometimes mistaken for being older.

His writings showed his plan was to give food to the children before kidnapping and killing them. The Beaumonts were in the age group of the victims Percy wanted to abduct and they went missing from the beach, as did Yvonne Tuohy, Marianne Schmidt, Christine Sharrock and Linda Stilwell. They were also taken from the front of the local yacht club. Percy was fascinated by sailing boats.

Certainly there are some elements of the general description that fitted but just as many that didn't. The original sketch of the suspect was done by a non-police artist and is not considered reliable.

Then was Percy there? He told police he had been to Adelaide on holiday but couldn't remember the date. His brother confirmed they had been there with his family. One of Percy's friend's mother told police: 'I can also recall that Derek travelled to Adelaide on holidays by plane on one occasion.'

When asked by detectives from Operation Heats detectives in 2005 if he was in Adelaide when the Beaumonts went missing he answered: 'I don't know.'

They then asked if he were blocking out thoughts 'because something horrible happened in Adelaide and you don't want to remember it?'

He eventually acknowledged: 'It's possible.'

Five days after the Tuohy murder Percy was interviewed by prison psychiatrist Doctor Allen Bartholomew, who found the young man had the capacity to repress memories of crimes he'd committed. He said that if Percy had been arrested a week after the murder he would no longer have been able to recall what he had done.

Now Percy says he can't remember when he was in Adelaide, but back in 1969 when he was talking to his old school friend in the Russell Street cells, he admitted he had been in Adelaide when the Beaumonts went missing: 'I was in Adelaide at the time.'

Percy was asked: 'Whereabouts were you, when they disappeared?'

'Near the beach. But nothing else.'

Without bodies or a confession Percy will remain on a short list of suspects for the Beaumont children. There is simply insufficient evidence to prove or disprove his involvement.

Detective Sergeant Brian Swan from Adelaide's major crime investigation branch said Percy 'remains a person of interest in the disappearance of the Beaumont children'.

Police from Operation Heats have been able to independently corroborate much of what Percy said to his policeman friend in the Russell Street watch-house.

So the question remains, why would he have lied about being on an Adelaide beach at the precise time the Beaumonts disappeared?

As Dr Bartholomew observed after interviewing Percy: 'It is not beyond the bounds of possibility that there is some other great harm been done in the past and there is no way of knowing it.'

ON September 27, 1966, Allen Geoffrey Redston, 6, left his home in the Canberra suburb of Curtin to go to the nearby milk bar to buy an ice-cream.

The following day his body was discovered concealed in reeds beside a local creek, wrapped in a floral housecoat and mushroom-coloured carpet. The little boy had been hogtied and there was plastic wrapped around his throat.

A police investigation found that in the days leading up to the murder a blond-haired teenager had been forcing boys to the ground, tying them up and placing plastic over their heads in an apparent attempt to asphyxiate them.

The identikit image is remarkably similar to Percy and the suspect was reported to be riding a distinctive red bike with 'ram's horn' handlebars – the type Percy rode at Mount Beauty and took with him on caravan holidays.

When Dick Knight questioned Percy back in 1969 the suspect said he had been on a family holiday in Canberra in 1966 but he was vague about details.

Police have established Percy had a relative who lived in the ACT but have found no records to pinpoint the exact date of the holiday. In the era before credit cards, automatic cash machines and closed circuit security cameras, people left far fewer signs behind them, making investigation years after the trail had gone cold particularly difficult.

But there were some clues pointing to a connection between the killer and the Canberra child's murder. Percy's writings, seized at Cerberus, detail the use of plastic and his plans to tie up and asphyxiate victims.

The bodies of both little Allen Redston and Yvonne Tuohy were tied and gagged when their bodies were found.

No-one will ever know why Percy became a child killer. He had an apparently normal childhood and was the product of an otherwise stable family. So what was the key that unlocked the hidden evil?

The family secret was that when Derek Percy was young and being cared for by his grandmother she would use a bizarre form of punishment. If she thought he had been naughty she would lock him in a room by himself. But first she would hogtie him – just like someone did to Allen Redston.

There was one other item found at the Canberra crime scene that puzzled the original investigators. Along with plastic, rope and cloth used to bind the victim, was a tattered green and gold diagonally-striped tie.

It had a similar colour and pattern to the ties worn by students at Mount Beauty High School but it was a little different to the school tie – it was made of rough hessian fabric, just like the one Percy had worn to school. No-one knows what happened to the school tie after he transferred to Corryong High earlier that year and didn't need it any more. No-one except Derek Percy, and if he remembers, he's not talking.

Federal police now say Percy 'cannot be completely eliminated as a person of interest in relation to the death'. It seems a conservative conclusion.

AFTER three months in the navy, Percy was posted to the aircraft carrier HMAS *Melbourne* on March 9, 1968 – but the flagship was in Cockatoo Dry Dock in Sydney Harbour for a year-long refit and the junior sailor was assigned simple fire sentry duty.

He lived at the naval base, Kuttabul, at nearby Garden Island and commuted through the suburb of Glebe to the dock. He knew the area well, as the previous year he had visited his father who was completing a Shell training course in Glebe before taking over a NSW service station.

On Saturday May 18, 1968, Simon Brook, 3, went missing from his family home in Alexandra Road, Glebe. His parents last saw him playing in the front yard. When they went outside after having coffee with friends he was gone. The house was next to Jubilee Park on Sydney Harbour – close to the beach and yachts.

A truck driver later came forward to say he had seen a boy matching Simon Brook's description holding the hand of a young man near Jubilee Park. He described the man as well groomed with a neat haircut.

Police say the identikit has a striking resemblance to a photo of Percy taken from his school year book.

Simon Brook's body was found at the rear of a block of flats being constructed at Glebe Point Road, Glebe – about 350 metres from the Brooks' family home.

There were several signature similarities to the fatal injuries inflicted on Yvonne Tuohy. When police examined the scene they found two Gillette Super Stainless brand razor blades they believed were used in the attack. The same brand was issued to sailors at navy bases.

Again the most damning evidence comes from Percy's own hand. In his green diary, seized by police at Cerberus, he wrote of abducting and killing a three-year-old 'baby'. He also described in sickening detail the exact injuries inflicted on Simon Brook. Operation Heats detectives say it is tantamount to a confession.

When Victorian detective Dick Knight interviewed Percy back in 1969 he asked: 'Did you kill Simon Brook?' The suspect responded: 'I could have.'

And when Percy talked to the old school friend policeman,

just days after he was arrested for the Tuohy murder, he admitted he was in the area at the time 'turning off at the railway cutting where the body was found'.

Only someone with a detailed knowledge of the area would know that Simon Brook lived near a railway cutting and if Percy 'turned off at the railway cutting' he would have driven straight past the Brooks' small street – and was quite possibly able to see the child playing in the front yard.

Another witness who lived in the area came forward at the time, claiming she saw Simon Brook on his own in the street next to his home that day.

She told police she told him to 'go inside because it was cold'. She said the boy ran up Alexandra Road to Victoria Street.

If Percy had turned off at the railway cutting as he said he would have had to drive along Victoria Street on the day of the abduction.

There can be no doubt by the time Percy had joined the navy he had graduated to being a serial predator.

Shortly after joining the navy Percy returned to Mount Beauty to visit friends. During the visit his car broke down and he took the younger brother of a mate for the fifteen-minute walk to the service station. During the walk he began to ask the six-year-old inappropriate questions about his two sisters but the boy was too young to understand the danger.

When police seized Percy's diary they found he was planning to abduct the two sisters – again near water – at the Mount Beauty pondage.

After examining the evidence crime profiler Detective Senior Sergeant Debra Bennett concluded: 'It is my opinion there is all likelihood that the offender for Simon Brook's murder and the offender for Yvonne Tuohy's murder is one and the same.'

And NSW Coroner John Abernethy agreed. A new inquest

into Simon Brook's death was held in 2005 and after just two days he found the evidence so compelling he closed the hearing and referred the case to the Director of Public Prosecutions. Percy was flown to the inquest but chose not to give evidence on the grounds of self-incrimination.

Mr Abernethy said he believed there was a 'reasonable prospect ... that a jury would convict a known person in relation to the offence'.

LINDA Stilwell was only four when her family left Hampshire in England, sailing on the old Sitmar migrant ship the MV *Fairsky*. They arrived in Melbourne in April 1965.

Linda was the second youngest of four children. For her mother Jean and father Brian the new start in a new country could not save their marriage.

In July 1968, Brian left for New Zealand with their youngest child, Laura. Jean stayed in Melbourne with the remaining three. She found a job working at an Albert Park hotel and the family moved into a flat in nearby Beaconsfield Parade, Middle Park.

On Saturday August 10, 1968, Mrs Stilwell had to dash to buy groceries – shops closed at midday on Saturdays in the 1960s – and she told her children to stay home while she was gone.

But the temptation of the nearby beach was too much for the two oldest who wanted to explore their still-new neighbourhood. When Mrs Stilwell arrived home about midday, Karen aged eleven, and Gary, nine, had left. She dressed seven-year-old Linda, and told her to go and find her brother and sister to bring them home for lunch.

Three hours later Karen wandered home, announcing that Gary and Linda were fishing on the nearby St Kilda Pier.

Around 4pm Gary returned, saying Linda had gone to Little Luna Park to 'look at the rifles' with some boys. She sent her son back to find her sister but he came back saying he thought she might have gone to the local police station to collect some fishing rods.

Mrs Stilwell rang the police and was told that two boys had been in to get the rods but there was no sighting of a little girl.

It was several hours before police went to her house and realised this was more than a case of a wandering child. They launched an immediate search but Linda was never seen again.

The three small boys, aged seven, nine and ten, who Linda had been playing with told police they had last seen her at Little Luna Park.

Two days later, a woman contacted police and said she had seen a girl matching Linda Stilwell's description rolling down a grassy hill near the Lower Esplanade. She said she saw a man near the girl. She described him as about 30, with a dark olive complexion, thin features and wearing dark clothing.

She would tell police: 'The man was wearing a deep navy blue almost black spray jacket, similar to that worn when sailing. The jacket was similar in appearance to what was referred to as a slicker. The man was sitting with his legs crossed looking out to sea quite intently, but appeared relaxed.'

Over the next few months about 80 suspects were questioned but no real leads were ever established. Back then Percy was not on the list as he was unknown. Now police say he is the only credible suspect.

Percy transferred to the troop ship, HMAS *Sydney*, based in Melbourne, on July 1, 1968, but was on leave for eighteen days from August 5.

The victim was abducted from the beach and near yachts, consistent with the pattern identified as Percy's modus operandi for murder. While the description of the suspect's sharp features also fitted, the suspect was said to look about 30 years old.

But when the policeman schoolmate saw Percy at the army

graduation of a mutual friend at Portsea in 1969 he was struck by how much his schoolmate had changed. 'At first I didn't recognise Derek and I can recall seeing him and thinking to myself, he has aged at least ten years.'

After Percy was arrested over the Tuohy murder the woman witness opened the paper to see the picture of the suspect on page one. He was wearing a dark spray jacket.

'I got the biggest shock of my life,' she was to say. 'This was the same man that was sitting on the park bench the day that the little Stilwell girl disappeared in St Kilda.'

Later she said she spoke to a detective who told her the man would never be released.

But, about two years ago, when Percy's arrest photo was again in the media and he was identified as a suspect in a series of unsolved murders, the witness came forward again.

'I am absolutely sure that the man I saw sitting on the park bench, the day Stilwell disappeared, is the same man.'

When asked by his policeman friend about the Stilwell disappearance in 1969 Percy said, 'Yes, I drove through St Kilda that day'. Asked directly if he killed her he said, 'Possibly, I don't remember a thing about it'.

When police searched his belongings they found a series of road maps with markings on them. One was in West Ryde near where the Wanda Beach victims hopped on the train, one was marked through the Glebe district where Simon Brook was killed and another was marked with a line to the Esplanade where Linda Stilwell was last seen.

Forty years ago police used identikits – an American identification method consisting of 365 small plastic overlays spread over twelve facial categories.

Witnesses were encouraged to help build a likeness using the available plastic pieces.

The head of the Victoria Police criminal identification squad,

Detective Sergeant Adrian Paterson, examined the old identikit images from the Wanda Beach, Simon Brook and Allen Redston cases.

He found there was a 'high probability' it was the same man. He examined them against photos of Percy taken at the times of the crimes and found them 'consistently similar'.

The identikits were produced by different experts, in different cities using different witnesses. But there is no doubt they all look like Percy at the time the crimes were committed.

Whenever Linda Stilwell's mother, now Jean Priest, moved house she would go to the homicide squad to pass on her new address, still hoping that one day she would get the call that there had been a breakthrough in the case.

But over the years she found the new generation of detectives no longer even recognised the name of her daughter and she knew the file had been forgotten.

But Operation Heats has given her new hope. 'It has helped me to know that people like (Senior Detective) Wayne Newman have cared so much and done so much work.'

Now a grandmother, and still with the soft English voice of her youth, she says, 'You learn to live with what has happened but you can never forget.'

She says Linda was always a wanderer who loved to explore and had no fear of strangers. 'She was happy and bright and would always find people to play with. She just loved everybody.'

Mrs Priest said she wanted the evidence against Percy produced at the Coroner's Inquest.

'Then I will be able to put a name to the face. It could finally bring some closure. I just hope he would finally admit what he has done.'

But she knows that after four decades of silence Percy is unlikely to change.

DEREK Percy was surprisingly talkative when Operation Heats investigators questioned him in the Melbourne homicide squad office in February 2005.

After all it was a day out and after 36 years in prison there were few events that broke the daily monotony of the regimented jail routine.

He had aged relatively well. Balding, with a long grey beard, he retained his striking cold blue stare and lean build. He chatted happily while drinking tea with three sugars and nibbling on a cheese and tomato sandwich from the police canteen.

Percy now spends much of his time collecting cricket statistics and remembers details from the games past but he still has trouble with his own memory.

He is serving an indefinite sentence under the insanity verdict but he has previously applied for a minimum term – an appeal that has been knocked back because he is still considered a danger to the community.

He still hopes to be released and a confession that he had killed many times would destroy his dreams.

Having received a navy pension since his arrest he is one of the richest inmates in the system with almost $200,000 in the bank.

Operation Heats detectives were to ask him 1535 questions. He could recall details of his childhood but when asked about the murders he would retreat within himself.

NSW Detective Sergeant Adam Barwick said when Percy was asked about the Brook murder he, 'was visibly different, in that his lip quivered, and his answer was "I can't remember". I formed the opinion that Percy was lying when answering these questions.'

Police believe that Percy's repeated answers that he cannot remember stem from self-protection rather than self-deception.

In other words Derek Ernest Percy is bad – not mad.

But detectives say the charade that he was insane at the time of the crimes is worth maintaining. If he had stood trial in 1970 for the murder of Yvonne Tuohy he would have been released years ago after serving his sentence and would have inevitably struck again.

Tom Attrill, the inspector who knew Percy when they were in the navy together in the late 1960s, was called in as an adviser to the Heats investigation.

He says the child killer hasn't changed and remains as dangerous as ever.

'I have no doubt that if he ever gets loose he will do it again. After 35 years in the job I would like to think I have a handle on people and nothing has changed with Percy except he has learned to play the game better.

'He is a disaster waiting to happen. He is highly intelligent, one of the most intelligent people I've met. He is cold, without emotion and looks straight through you with his crazy eyes.'

Mr Attrill said many former sailors were disgusted that Percy received a navy pension and had become wealthy while in jail.

He said it was vital that Percy remain in custody.

'The only way he should be allowed out is in a pine box,' Inspector Attrill said.

For investigators the problem remains that the crimes were so long ago and the children who could identify him are all dead.

But there is one woman who remembers.

She was just a girl in the 1960s but like most children of her generation she was given the freedom to explore on her bike as long as she was home at a reasonable hour.

She lived on the Mornington Peninsula and although she was only twelve her father warned her to be wary of the sailors stationed nearby at Cerberus. 'We would laugh at that because Dad used to be in the navy.'

Then one day around Easter 1969, (just a few months before Yvonne Tuohy was abducted at a nearby beach) she was riding along a dirt track when she realised a man in a cream-coloured panel van was following her. She said she cut across country but the van caught up with her in another street.

The driver asked her for directions 'with a pathetic little lost boy voice'.

The girl thought he was a sailor because of his short brown hair and because she saw navy stickers on the car and one with the words 'Go Navy or Go something on it'.

She said the driver cut her off and asked her to hop in his car to show him the way home. 'I was very scared at this stage because he was only a short distance from the Cerberus Naval Base and I thought to myself that he knows exactly where he is.'

The girl pedalled into a driveway and screamed for help. The driver sped off.

A few weeks later, after Yvonne Tuohy was murdered, police seized Percy's cream-coloured van.

On the back window was a navy sticker. And on the side was one from his father's service station that read 'Go well – Go Shell'.

Thirty-five years later the woman, now a nurse, was working a nightshift in a nursing home when she saw a 1969 picture of Percy reprinted in a newspaper that instantly brought back memories.

She kept returning to look at the photo, wondering why the man looked familiar.

'It took two or three days for it to click into place. Then I knew the person on the front page was the same person who followed me all those years ago in Hastings.'

Police are certain her decision to pull into the driveway saved her from being another victim of the man who can't remember.

DEREK Ernest Percy may be a man who refuses to say what he thinks, but the suspected serial killer cannot help implicating himself by his own hand.

When questioned over the years of his suspected involvement in child killings his answers have always been the same: that he simply can't remember. No denials, no false alibis, just a blank look followed by a non-committal response.

In August 2007, after gaining an order from the Melbourne Magistrates Court, Victorian and NSW detectives again interviewed him over a series of abductions and murders that began in 1965 and stopped when he was arrested in 1969.

While he doesn't speak of his black past, his diaries have always documented his violent sexual obsessions. And it is that compulsion, which has given police a glimmer of hope of finding answers to some of Australia's most awful crimes.

The reason police moved to question him was that they had discovered Percy's secret: something he had hidden away in a nondescript South Melbourne storage depot for decades. Inside the unit Percy rented were 35 cardboard boxes and tea chests filled with his papers and possessions.

Much of what was found was innocuous enough – court records, transcripts and personal belongings. But a detailed search found a collection that would prove to be a window to Percy's black soul.

The material includes newspaper articles on sex crimes, pictures of children, a video with a rape theme and handwritten stories on fresh sex offences involving abduction and torture.

Percy managed to collect and transfer the material from jail to his private collection, despite being one of Australia's most violent sex criminals, judged too dangerous for release.

Police now know that Percy, a former naval rating, has maintained storage facilities in Melbourne since the early 1970s.

For two years after his arrest Percy was a model prisoner, but in September 1971 prison staff found he was writing about abductions and murders.

The elaborate plots he constructed included abducting one or both of a schoolmate's sisters in Mount Beauty: 'Go down below the lake and meet her on way. Tell her my car is bogged down there and I want help. Get her in car and take her to place,' he wrote.

When Percy began legal moves to push for his freedom in 1998 the Supreme Court was told: 'Since 1971 Mr Percy has never written anything which could be indicative of any sexual fantasy.'

But the discovery of his stored material shows that after the diaries were discovered in his cell Percy began to hide his writings and clippings by sending them out of the prison.

Police say the evidence he placed in storage indicates Percy has not changed: on the contrary, he deliberately hid incriminating material that would destroy his hopes for release.

'If he has stored them he must believe he will get out so he can recover them,' a senior policeman said.

Police say that Percy has moved material from prison since the early 1970s, first to a rented lock-up at Pascoe Vale and, for the past 20 years, to the South Melbourne self-store unit.

They found a 1978 street directory with a line drawn through the St Kilda Pier where Linda Stilwell was abducted 10 years earlier, and a pornographic lesbian cartoon on which Percy has written the word 'Wanda' across the top.

They also found razor blades similar to the type used to mutilate Simon Brook.

When Percy was arrested in 1969, police found that he had maps of the areas where Linda Stilwell, Christine Sharrock, Marianne Schmidt and Simon Brook lived or were murdered.

Among the items seized from the lock-up was a stamp collection valued at several thousand dollars that Percy had compiled in prison.

The first policeman to arrest Percy has no doubt he is a multiple killer. Alan Hyde was a senior constable in the wireless patrol in 1969 when he was called to the abduction at Warneet beach near Western Port.

He said that when they found the suspect at Cerberus 'We found Percy washing his gear that was still covered with blood'.

He said they opened Percy's locker and found 'reams and reams of paper where he had written what he wanted to do to kids and women'.

'We got him within two hours. If it had been two days, I believe he would have been able to put it out of his mind.'

Mr Hyde said he believed Percy killed Simon Brook, Christine Sharrock and Marianne Schmidt.

'The injuries were very similar to those inflicted on Yvonne Tuohy. I have no doubt he is the offender.

'He was very quiet and very cunning. If he was to be released, I have no doubt he would do the same thing again.'

In August 2007 a court finally officially found Linda Stilwell had been murdered. Magistrate Susan Wakeling granted the Stilwell family an application for crimes compensation, accepting Linda had been abducted and killed.

Linda's brother, Gary, urged Percy to confess. 'Our family has been traumatised enough and all we want is closure. I appeal to any shred of decency within Percy to come forward with any information he has so that we can find the remains of my sister.'

## Timeline

## Derek Ernest Percy

*1948, September 15:* Born in Strathfield, NSW.

*1954:* Attends primary school in Missions Point, NSW.

*1956*: Family moves to Chelsea.

*1958*: Family moves to Warrnambool.

*1961*: Family moves to Mount Beauty.

*1964*: Seen slashing women's clothing. Increasing reports of snowdropping in district. Percy is considered a suspect.

*1965, January 11:* Wanda Beach murders. Mount Beauty locals see resemblance between Percy and identikit of suspect.

*1965:* Starts keeping graphic diary. School grades plummet. Fails Leaving certificate.

*1966*: Moves to Khancoban. Molests young girl. The crime is not reported to police.

*1966, January 26:* Three Beaumont children go missing from the Glenelg beach. Mount Beauty residents recall Percy holidaying in Adelaide. Percy says he was in Adelaide on the beach on the day the children were abducted.

*1966, September 27:* Allen Geoffrey Redston, 6, is abducted and murdered in Canberra. Percy tells police he has holidayed in the capital but can't recall details. In the days leading up to the murder there are reports of a teenager attempting to suffocate children in the area. The description fits Percy. The suspect rode a bike similar to Percy's and the victim was bound with a tie similar to the Mount Beauty High School uniform tie.

*1967, November 25:* Percy joins navy.

*1968, March 9:* Stationed in Sydney.

*1968, May 18:* Simon Brook, 3, is abducted and murdered in Glebe. Percy writes in his diary of abducting and murdering a three-year-old. The details in the diary match the fatal injuries inflicted on the victim.

*1968, August 5:* Percy goes on eighteen days leave from navy. Tells police he stays in Melbourne.

*1968, August 10:* Linda Stilwell abducted from St Kilda foreshore. Percy was on leave at the time, had a map marked in the area she went missing and told police he was in the area on the day.

*1969, April 1:* Stationed at Cerberus.

*1969:* Probably attempted abduction of a twelve-year-old girl on a bike near the Cerberus base. Victim later identifies Percy as a suspect.

*1969, July 27:* Abducts and murders Yvonne Tuohy from Ski Beach. Arrested later that day. Police find his diary filled with violent sex fantasies.

*1970:* Found not guilty of the Tuohy murder on the grounds of insanity.

# CHAPTER 3

# Playing on thin ice

One cocaine-using player told him more than half the team were into it. 'At first the club didn't want to believe it. Now they say "Our blokes do it – but they're no worse than any other club." They are kidding themselves .'

ELITE AFL players are young and rich, and often act as if they are above the law – but they are not invincible. A high-flying premiership player learned that the hard way in the spring of 2006 when he almost died in an American hospital.

The strange circumstances surrounding a super-fit professional athlete being revived after 'flatlining' is a story most football insiders know – but none talked about it publicly until the story was blown open in early 2007.

'Mate, it's right but they'd hang me off the grandstand if I went on the record,' a respected former player and official told one of the authors.

'It's such a small world, football.'

Like several other well-placed sources who confirmed the story, he made it clear that the game's unwritten code of silence ('what happens on the footy trip stays on the footy trip') was in this case reinforced with corporate spin and implied threats of reprisals against anyone who broke ranks.

The perceived risk of lawsuits has smothered all but the most oblique references to the mysterious medical emergency that could have ended with the player coming home from the end of season trip in a coffin. (Instead, he spent several days in hospital before being able to travel – and did not rejoin his team-mates.)

There are potent reasons for such an explosive scandal to stay 'in club'. The AFL and its sixteen clubs have much at stake: multi-million-dollar sponsorships could evaporate if the lucrative AFL 'brand' was damaged with one burst of bad publicity.

And publicity couldn't get much worse than exposure of what really happened in that Las Vegas hospital in late 2006.

On the record, players and club officials go along with the club's cryptic explanation dismissing the incident as a routine medical matter. Off the record, insiders have told friends and relatives their man overdosed.

This fits a pattern of misbehaviour by AFL players, and a tendency for clubs to cover up for those considered too valuable to lose. This comes at the expense, sometimes, of lesser lights axed to protect sponsorships and the game's billion-dollar brand image.

THE spectre of alcohol and substance abuse hangs over the Las Vegas episode as it hangs over other strange incidents – the arrest, for instance, of Geelong's Steve Johnson in Wangaratta in early 2007.

Worried householders called police after he staggered into their yard late at night and allegedly tried to drink from a bottle of suntan oil on their patio. (There is no suggestion that Johnson was anything but inebriated.)

Then there is the weird behaviour of Carlton's Brendan Fevola in attacking an Irish barman during a big night out after a winning day at the races during the 2006 tour of Ireland. This was eclipsed by Eagles midfielder Daniel Kerr's bizarre late-night attack on a Perth taxi driver outside a hospital where he had taken a friend after a sudden bout of illness in a nightspot. Kerr is unlucky like that – his girlfriend was already in hospital after suffering a seizure.

Kerr's erratic lifestyle is notorious even in a city where footballers' excesses are mostly forgiven by adoring fans, some of whom run AFL clubs. The sort of fans who supported Brownlow medallist Ben Cousins when he left his car on a busy highway and bolted to avoid a booze bus. And when he was found unconscious near Melbourne's casino after another long night – more of that later.

A young woman who went out with Kerr has told close friends she was shocked because he could not remember where he was – or who he was sleeping with – after he woke from 'a big night'.

One night over summer Kerr asked her to pick him up from a party (where he had been involved in a fight). When she arrived he looked at her blankly and said: 'Who are you? Are you my lift?' She stopped seeing him after that.

Another regular at Perth's nightspots told the authors that Kerr 'is constantly out of it and makes no secret of it. He sits around in bars and slurs his words. He doesn't recognise you from one day to the next'.

On December 16, 2006, one of Kerr's team-mates narrowly escaped being caught in a police raid on the Red Sea bar, where he had been drinking with members of the Coffin Cheaters motorcycle gang.

A well-known former Eagle was close friends with a champion dubbed 'the Cocaine Kid' – and shared his taste in drugs.

'Girls I know used to go around to his house and he would be snorting coke off the coffee table,' the woman said. 'One of the girls commented one night about a year ago, "Don't you have to play football?" and he said "Are you trying to break my balls?" '

At the time, the player acted like the gangsters he hung around with; now, he is reputedly trying to regain the promise he showed on the field, but still hangs around with a tough crew after hours.

There was a sinister element to the big man's edgy lifestyle: neighbours noticed people visiting his house at all times of night.

They were relieved when he moved out.

FOR all their on-field success, the Eagles have the worst reputation for drug and alcohol-fuelled misbehaviour. Other clubs have troubles – some inherited when they take on problem players 'released' by original clubs – but the Eagles are notorious for flying too high.

'Drugs are rife at West Coast,' a former club official declares. 'At first the club didn't want to believe it. Now they say, "Our blokes do it – but they're no worse than any other club". They are kidding themselves.'

One cocaine-using player told him more than half the team were 'into it', he says.

Worse, at least two club stars were 'into the super, whizz-bang stuff' so heavily that their supplier gave them other drugs to mask the effects of post-game binges. The supplier, he says, is a supporter keen to trade A-list 'party' drugs to rub shoulders with A-list players.

This person is not, as some might assume, well-known Perth identity John Kizon, although Kizon's socialising with key players has long caused heartburn for club officials.

West Coast was warned about the Kizon connection in 2001

when a police source tipped off the club that crime investigators had taped conversations linking Brownlow medallist Ben Cousins and the since-disgraced Michael Gardiner with underworld figures. (Gardiner was sacked by the Eagles after a high-speed car crash while drunk.)

The inference of a drug link was strong (if not necessarily true) as Kizon is a convicted heroin trafficker and has nightclub and entertainment interests.

The charismatic and calculating Kizon, a former boxer from Fitzroy who remains a fitness fanatic, was a friend of the late Alphonse Gangitano; he flew to Melbourne to be a pall bearer at the gangster's huge funeral after Gangitano was shot dead in early 1998.

He is close to the Coffin Cheaters – a gang whose influence is arguably greater in Perth than that of any outlaw gang in any other Australian city.

In Perth he is admired by some; feared by many. It was inevitable he would make contact with the local heroes, the Eagles. Gangsters and stars often find each other.

In Grand Final week, 2001, police saw Kizon meet Gardiner and Cousins at the Crown Casino complex; the three drank together at Fidel's Cigar Bar later that night.

Despite warnings, the two players did not distance themselves from Kizon; they were seen drinking with his Melbourne friends after an Eagles–Carlton game in early 2002. The Carlton connection is interesting, as the criminal Moran family – of which three members were killed in the underworld war – was closely connected to the club for three generations.

One of Carlton's great finals players reputedly played under the influence of drugs – 'his eyes would be rolling around like mad' recalls a contemporary – and later became a dealer among younger players.

He saw a Carlton player at a nightclub during the finals in the late 1990s and, while commiserating with him for being dropped from the side, slipped the embarrassed player some drugs. He is still reputed to deal to players – and he isn't the only one.

THREE years ago, Carlton recruits Laurence Angwin and Karl Norman were exiled from AFL football for turning up to a morning 'recovery' session under the influence of ecstasy. Angwin now plays for South Cairns, Norman with Mooroopna in country Victoria.

Carlton is quick to discredit Angwin because of his troubled history but his story has not changed.

Originally from interstate, he claims AFL players in Melbourne introduced him to ecstasy.

'There would have been eight blokes (Carlton players) there that day who wouldn't have passed a test. Five out of the nine in the leadership group couldn't make eye contact with us when they called us in because they'd been out with us. You can't hit a circle of footballers where there's not something going around.'

Angwin's point is backed by a former AFL coach of impeccable character and high standing. He tells the story of a Crows star (with reputed shady connections) taking a fishing tackle box on a team trip. Inside it were not hooks and sinkers, just dozens of brightly coloured pills. Drugs.

That might disappoint some club officials but it won't shock them.

Having taught players that drinking shows up in skinfold tests, they're now coping with a relentless rise in drug use. Drugs might fry your brain or stop your heart but they don't put on weight and, for young risk-takers on big money looking for a good time, that's a big attraction. Clubs are getting nervous about this.

In fact, there's already a quiet move to reverse the collateral damage done by the push against drinking. A former coach says some clubs are quietly reviving the practice of players having a few drinks after the game.

'Don't worry too much about the skinfolds – we'll work it off on the track' is the attitude. Just like the old days.

But it's hard for some to go back to the mild side after walking the wild side. One All-Australian player who made too much of his days in the sun, boasted brazenly to a club official: 'You haven't lived until you've had (a beauty queen) snort coke off your d—'

The beauty queen is going well, but the player's career is in ruins.

THE West Coast Eagles should not delude themselves that 'eastern staters' are out to get them or their football code. If that were the case, explain the kind action of a Melbourne soccer player who rescued a dazed and confused Ben Cousins from a street corner in December, 2006, hours before the Brownlow medallist was photographed unconscious outside Crown Casino and later taken into custody by police.

It happened a little after 2am on Saturday, December 2, when the good samaritan stopped at a traffic light near the casino and saw a young man standing in the street 'shivering'.

'I asked him if he was all right and he walked towards the car and I realised it was Ben Cousins,' he said later.

Cousins is renowned for being able to run all day – and a long way at night to avoid a booze bus – but this time the iron man of the midfield could hardly move.

Cousins was so 'out of it', the social soccer player – and Aussie rules fan – later told friends, that he offered him a lift to get him off the street for fear he would be run over.

Cousins waved a $50 note and mumbled that he wanted to go

'back to' Eve nightclub, a few hundred metres away, and threw himself into the back seat of the car.

The 30-year-old driver, who did not want to be identified, says he was shocked and concerned at Cousins' distressed condition.

'He was sweating and paranoid. He had his hands over his face and was looking around as if he was frightened someone was chasing him. He said someone had hit him – he pulled up his shirt and showed me his stomach. He was jumping all over the back seat. I think I can tell the difference between being drunk and drugs and I'd say he was tripping out bad – his brain was fried on some hard-core stuff, I'd say.'

Cousins was aware of his condition and concerned about being recognised, the driver said.

'I had a girl with me who didn't recognise him until I said his name and then he said, "No, no. It's not me!" He stayed in the car about five minutes, talking. I really gave it to him. I said, "What are you doing, ruining your career, mate?" And he said, "No drugs, no drugs, I don't want that".'

The driver took him to the nightclub from where Cousins had claimed, he had been 'chased' earlier.

'I don't know if someone really chased him or not,' he said. When the driver politely refused his offer of payment, Cousins thrust a $10 note at him, got out and walked unsteadily towards the casino.

That was the last the driver saw of him until a photograph of his famous passenger appeared in the newspapers two days later. Someone had caught Cousins 'asleep' on the ground near the casino before the police came and locked him up for four hours.

The friendly soccer player still has the $10 as a memento of his brush with celebrity. He is not the only person who likes being around famous sports people.

# PLAYING ON THIN ICE

According to a former head of the Victorian drug squad, John McKoy, footballers can be victims of the appeal they hold for 'ordinary' people, including some of the most ordinary of all – drug dealers and gangsters.

McKoy, who spent eleven years in the drug squad before retiring as a detective chief inspector in 2000, said elite footballers had to be careful because drug dealers liked to cultivate high-profile people.

'They target celebrities like footballers and entertainers.'

He said the link between footballers and drugs went back a long way. 'In the past, detectives came across some prominent footballers on the fringe of major drug investigations.

'We didn't pursue them any more vigorously than anyone else.'

But he confirmed persistent rumours that some players crossed the line.

A famous and much-loved larrikin Collingwood player acted as a bodyguard and standover man for an amphetamines dealer who was later killed in a road crash. And a failed league ruckman became a drug dealer who for years displayed more speed in his hip pocket than he had ever shown in the forward pocket.

Another former drug squad detective was astonished to discover that several players in a suburban football competition, in which he had played and later coached, took ecstasy and amphetamines at weekends.

'When I returned to my club to coach after five years away, I found that a lot of players were on the stuff on Saturday nights and would be awake all weekend. I'd be going to work at the drug squad Monday to Friday to catch blokes like Mokbel and the Morans and players in my own comp were buying their product.'

Former AFL coach Damian Drum, now a Victorian state MP,

warned the AFL three years ago that substance abuse was part of a hedonistic lifestyle that threatened to wreck young players' lives.

'I wrote a three-page letter to (AFL chief executive) Andrew Demetriou after the Canterbury Bulldogs (sexual assault) case, warning him that our boys would be next,' Drum told the authors.

'Most of them have too much money and time on their hands. While they are playing they are treated like gods and then they're tossed aside. It's not good for them.

'It's an unhealthy lifestyle in the present – and it doesn't prepare them for the future.

'We can't make them all work, but we could at least make them qualified.

'Players should be either full-time students or learn a trade so that they come out with a qualification – and the AFL should look at the US college sports scholarship system as a model.

'In America, sports scholarship holders have to get up early and do their academic work until early afternoon, then they meet their coaches and then they train. After dinner, they study again. Of about 80 at each college, only three or so make it to the top level – but they all have a qualification to go on with.'

Being educated meant players and athletes would mix with people outside the hothouse of elite sport, which would inject 'a sense of reality' into players' lives.

Young players, especially, can be left in a vacuum and have to kill time outside training hours in any way they like. The result, says Drum wryly, is that 'the only qualification they get is a degree in PlayStation 3'.

A WEEK after Damian Drum made his warning, Melbourne's *Sunday Age* newspaper broke the story that one of Australian football's biggest stars was under discreet investigation by drug squad police as part of a wide-ranging inquiry into a so-called 'rat-pack' of cocaine users in sport, media and entertainment.

And, much to the satisfaction of the West Coast club, he is not (and never was) an Eagle.

The former star of a Melbourne-based club has maintained a high profile in the media since his retirement from the game he played with distinction.

Persistent rumours of his links with a drug dealer prompted detectives to monitor his activities in early 2007.

The result, according to a well-placed source, is that the colourful football identity has unwittingly led investigators to the dealer, allowing them to gather evidence that could be used to lay charges.

It was understood police planned to recruit a third person known to the football identity to help an undercover detective to infiltrate a 'rat-pack' of sporting and media people who regularly use cocaine.

'People in his (the football identity's) position should be careful what they tell the hairdresser,' the source said. 'Hairdressers do not tend to keep secrets under questioning.'

The group reputedly buys thousands of dollars worth of the illicit drug from a favoured dealer each week. Police did not set out to target the members of the group but have used them to set a trap for the 'dealer to the stars', the source said.

'The coppers haven't spoken to him just yet but he is high on the list,' the source said.

'It's called arrest by appointment: he will soon be invited in to the major drug investigation unit for a cup of tea and a teddy bear biscuit.

'He will then either be charged or will help the police with their inquiries into the dealer. The way to put pressure on the dealer is to put pressure on his customers and get them to lag him in. The drug squad will get statements from the customers to nail the big guy.'

The high-profile cocaine user will be faced with either supplying information against the dealer or risking charges himself.

The investigation uncovered the existence of a luxury 'love boat'. The multi-million-dollar pleasure craft is used for weekend cruises on the bay to which selected 'guests' pay up to $5000 for unlimited cocaine and sex with escorts. Current and former AFL players – and media 'players' – are believed to be among those who have used the boat.

The secret police investigation was another episode in a turbulent season for football off the field in 2007, following revelations about the extent of drug abuse among AFL players.

The uproar over the admission that Eagles star and Brownlow medallist Ben Cousins was dangerously addicted to 'ice' (crystal methamphetamine) has affected football followers from the cheer squad to AFL headquarters and the Prime Minister's office.

Prime Minister John Howard said on Melbourne radio he favoured 'zero tolerance' towards all illicit drugs inside or outside sport.

And AFL chief executive Andrew Demetriou used the AFL's 2007 season launch in March to promise support for Cousins and his family for the player's rehabilitation.

This foreshadowed Cousins being sent to an expensive drug clinic in Los Angeles for a month before being allowed to resume with the Eagles in late July.

The media frenzy over the story prompted speculation that several other West Coast players also abused illicit drugs.

The manager of one West Coast player was so concerned at rumours that he took the unusual step of contacting a newspaper to say that if any story were published about his client without 'stat decs, video evidence and an affidavit from his mother' then he would sue for damages.

West Coast coach John Worsfold eventually revealed that Daniel Kerr was one of up to eight Eagles players who had admitted taking recreational drugs.

'I would suggest that it would be half a dozen, maybe eight players, that have admitted they have used an illicit drug – but we are certainly not talking about drug problems,' Worsfold said.

# CHAPTER 4

# Blood on the streets

If they were not outlaw bikies many would be just overweight, middle-aged men with no career prospects, few life skills and chronic body odour …

THE bikies had every reason to hate Don Hancock. They knew the former senior Perth detective turned country publican had shot dead a Gypsy Joker member called Billy Grierson after a minor dispute in October 2000.

By the time police got to Hancock he was showered and changed. The stickler for police procedure refused to hand over his original clothing, defied instructions to stay at the scene and then ate an orange to remove gunshot residue.

Investigating police believed Hancock was the sniper who shot Grierson that night in the West Australian goldfields town of Ora Banda.

The Gypsy Jokers believed Hancock, former head of the CIB, was not charged because the reputation of an ex-policeman was more important than a bikie's life.

They vowed revenge – and then went to war. They repeatedly bombed Hancock's pub and home – concealing the explosives before one attack in the coffin of a teenage boy.

Hancock – known as the Silver Fox – knew he was a marked man and returned to Perth where a state-of-the art security system was set up in his home.

Although retired he was allowed to carry a handgun because of the constant threat to his life.

But video cameras and a .38 revolver would never be enough to protect the 64-year-old former policeman.

For months the bikies tried to follow Hancock without getting close enough to kill him but they soon found his weakness. The former old-school copper was a creature of habit who regularly went to the races with a mate, retired bookie Lou Lewis.

When Gypsy Jokers were leaked the details of the bookie's car by a tame source within the WA Transport Department the rest was easy.

Gang members strolled around the Belmont Park racecourse until they found Lewis' unlocked car and then gently slipped a bomb under the passenger seat.

As the two men drove home on September 1, 2001, one of the bikies used a mobile phone (as terrorists often do) to trigger the ammonium nitrate bomb, muttering 'Rest in peace, Billy' before the bomb detonated, obliterating both victims.

The explosion was heard more than eight kilometres away. The ramifications would last for years.

Don Hancock was their enemy but Lou Lewis was not involved. To the bikies he was just acceptable collateral damage.

Welcome to the world of outlaw motorcycle gangs, where violence is often the first and only resort.

ON June 18, 2007, as Melbourne's morning rush was peaking, behind closed doors in the so-called entertainment district centred on King Street, some were still coming down from the night before.

A stripper from Spearmint Rhino, Autumn Daly-Holt, was dancing provocatively next door in Bar Code. Then she was bashed savagely, allegedly by a member of the Hell's Angels motorcycle gang.

The bikie, Christopher Wayne Hudson, was alleged to have then jumped in a taxi with another stripper, Kaera Douglas, 24. As they argued the cab pulled up at the corner of Flinders Lane and William Street.

Witnesses said a man, later identified as Hudson, tried to drag her from the car.

Two men, solicitor Brendan Keilar, 43, and Paul de Waard, a 25-year-old Dutch backpacker, tried to step in. Keilar was shot and died in the street. De Waard and Douglas were also shot and seriously injured.

Witnesses said the gunman hesitated then pointed the gun under his own chin as if considering suicide. But self-preservation instincts over-rode the impulse and he dumped the gun before escaping.

The obscene violence that morning graphically exposed what happens when Melbourne's underbelly of guns, drugs and vice collides with the mainstream world on a busy city street.

And while the rampage cannot be blamed on the Hell's Angels – it appeared to be a domestic dispute gone mad – it raises questions about the bikie culture and the community's response to the ever-present threat.

The Australian Crime Commission says there are seventeen outlaw motorcycle gangs in Victoria, and 35 throughout Australia, with a total of 3500 fully-patched members and perhaps as many again who are associates.

The ACC is investigating bikie groups as established criminal networks, and has connected them with prolific money laundering, tax fraud, firearms trafficking and drug manufacturing.

The commission has found that the 'size, profile, geographic spread and level of sophistication of OMCG (outlaw motorcycle gangs) criminal activity presents a significant threat to Australia and its interests'.

It says gangs infiltrate legitimate business enterprises, 'including finance, transport, private security, entertainment, natural resources and construction'.

There is nothing subtle about outlaw bikies. While many gangsters try to conceal their underworld connections behind closed penthouse doors, bikies wear their colours to show their criminal spots.

It is a deliberate strategy designed to forge military-style loyalty between members while simultaneously intimidating outsiders.

Some brag they are like a swarm of bees that will attack (and die) to protect the hive.

The analogy has some substance. Most of the bikies are like worker bees. They do not share in the massive profits but get their identity from the collective.

If they were not outlaw bikies many would be just overweight, middle-aged men with no career prospects, few life skills and chronic body odour.

But those who rise to run the clubs often have affluent lifestyles and manage to run successful businesses – suspected of being fronts to launder drug money. Bikies have also moved into debt collecting, using their fearsome reputations to stand over parties in civil disputes.

They have been known to wear their gang colours to auctions – a move designed to intimidate rival bidders.

The outlaw bikie world remains in a constant state of tension, with smaller clubs at risk of violent takeover by the Hell's Angels, Bandidos, Rebels, Outlaws, Black Uhlans and Nomads.

Police in Sydney are facing bikie violence as gangs battle to gain control of the lucrative nightclub drug scene. In the same week as the Melbourne CBD shooting a bomb exploded outside a Hell's Angels clubhouse in Sydney. Similar battles have broken out in Queensland.

Unlike the Melbourne underworld war, in which victims were shot in ambushes, the Finks and Hell's Angels went to war within a crowd of 1600 people at a kickboxing event on the Gold Coast.

In Geelong the Rebels' headquarters were firebombed in April 2007 and the Bandidos' clubhouse was sprayed with bullets.

Earlier that month two gunmen shot four Rebels gang members in an Adelaide nightclub.

Police say outlaw gangs in Australia have been bullying their way into nightclub ownership, club security, strippers, entertainment, modelling agencies and prostitution. They have attempted to buy a legal brothel using associates with no criminal records as a front.

In Melbourne, while bikies do not appear to own nightclubs – at least on paper – police intelligence shows gang associates own, run and control security at some venues.

Police say rival bikie gangs are trying to gain control of security at popular venues so they can green-light the distribution of their drugs through sanctioned dealers.

'Control the front door and you control who gets in. Control who gets in and you control the distribution of drugs,' according to one veteran investigator.

In Victoria, bikie headquarters are easily identified and heavily protected.

The Special Operations Group has used bulldozers, a ram-truck and explosives to gain access. In Western Australia special anti-fortification laws have been passed to try to stop bikies building domestic forts in Perth.

In the 1980s an Australian Bureau of Criminal Intelligence investigation into bikies codenamed Wingclipping found the gangs to be a serious organised crime threat.

And the problems have only escalated in the past two decades. In *Angels of Death: Inside the Bikers Global Crime Empire*, Canadian experts William Marsden and Julian Sher say Australia has the highest number of bikies per capita in the world.

Marsden and Sher found that since the mid-1990s Australian bikies have been locked in a decade-long battle to control their slice of the massive drug market. 'Over the next five years, 32 bik es would die and many more would be beaten as the Hell's Angels, Bandidos and other clubs fought over the amphetamine trade.'

In fact it was in the mid-1970s that the Hell's Angels pioneered the trade in Australia – and first established the international nature of Bikie Inc.


PETER John Hill was not an average bikie. The former private school boy and son of a bank executive loved motorbikes and became an original Melbourne Hell's Angel.

Hill became friendly with senior Californian Angels, including hitman James Patton 'Jim Jim' Brandes.

When Hill visited the Oakland Chapter, Brandes took him to prison to meet the gang's amphetamine expert – Kenny 'KO' Walton.

Walton told Hill how to make speed and later mailed him a detailed recipe. In return Melbourne Hell's Angels organised to smuggle a vital ingredient for amphetamine production to the US gang.

At the time the chemical P2P was difficult to source in the US but remained freely available in Australia.

Hill and his team filled three-litre Golden Circle pineapple tins with the chemical and mailed them, two at a time, to the Oakland chapter.

After 50 deliveries the Californian gang had sufficient to make $US50 million in speed.

Bob Armstrong was the Victorian policeman who would spend half a career in investigations, surveillance and undercover work that centred on the bikies. His original team smashed the Hell's Angels Greenslopes amphetamines lab in 1982, finding three kilograms of speed, cash, handguns and a machine-gun.

Later he received a call from Peter Hill's mother, Audrey, telling the detective that a US hitman was on his way to kill him.

The suspect was grabbed as he walked from his plane into Melbourne Airport.

It was 'Jim Jim' Brandes, who had previously seriously injured an American detective after setting off a bomb next to the policeman's car.

Peter Hill later fell out with the Angels and in an act of revenge he sold the original speed recipe to a rival gang for just $1000.

That gang was the Black Uhlans, whose founding members included the ambitious John William Samuel Higgs, later to become the biggest speed producer in Australia.

Higgs was in constant trouble with the police as a teenager, with his first conviction recorded at thirteen. He later gathered convictions as varied as manslaughter and the illegal possession of a stuffed possum.

Higgs was to become wildly rich and showed his gratitude to his gang by donating its Melbourne clubhouse. In return he was made a life member.

Higgs was the target of eight National Crime Authority, federal and Victorian Police operations from 1985, including

Australia's longest-running drug investigation, codenamed *Phalanx*. This eight-year inquiry led to the arrest of 135 people and the seizure of chemicals with the potential to make speed valued at $200 million.

The money made by select bikies places them squarely on the A-list of crime.

The investment portfolio of some gangs is vast.

Police say some have invested heavily in natural resources, including Australian mining and Indonesian oilrigs.

One illiterate ex-labourer and former bouncer known as the 'Maltese Falcon' controlled a real estate portfolio worth $3.3 million, 70 motorcycles and two Rolls-Royces. Bikies have also infiltrated government departments to access confidential computer records.

Investigating hardcore bikie gangs is notoriously difficult. They are usually security conscious, rarely trust outsiders and use expendable 'hang-arounds' and 'prospects' to complete low-end criminal activities.

They often have signs plastered on phones to remind them they may be bugged – although recently several forgot and used the phone to try to organise a quick insurance scam. The slip-up resulted in a successful prosecution.

They also have professionals electronically 'sweep' their clubhouses after police raids looking for listening devices. Routinely police find hot leads peter out when witnesses go cold.

A tow-truck driver who removed a bikie's vehicle seized by police was later bashed. A safe expert who opened a bikie safe after a police raid found his business badly damaged by fire.

One man who made a statement against a bikie was at first forced to move from Melbourne, and when he was threatened with a one-way trip to the cemetery, fled the country never to return.

One man who woke up in hospital after being tortured told police he had no idea what had happened.

Victoria's Chief Commissioner Christine Nixon defended the police response to bikie crime by saying the problem was greater in some other states.

'We are, in fact, working on these different bikie gangs. We are part of a whole national approach working on these bikie gangs.'

But some police disagree. The specialist bikie unit in the organised crime squad has been closed during a restructure. Some senior members of the crime squad want the decision reviewed.

It is difficult but not impossible to infiltrate bikie groups. Ten years ago two Victoria Police codenamed Wes and Alby went undercover for thirteen months to infiltrate the Bandidos as part of a secret operation codenamed *Operation Barkly*.

Alby and Wes were involved in more than 30 deals buying marijuana, amphetamines, LSD and ecstasy from Bandidos in three states.

They were so trusted that Alby became the secretary-elect for the Ballarat chapter, giving him access to the club's financial records.

Police eventually arrested twenty bikies as a result and uncovered plans for the gang to open nightclubs in Geelong and Ballarat as fronts for drug dealing.

*Operation Barkly* was closed because of the danger to the undercover police. During the investigation three Bandidos, including president Michael 'Chaos' Kulakowski, were murdered.

Bikies pride themselves on protecting and dealing with their own, but there is a limit.

The suspect in the CBD shooting was cut loose by the gang and had no choice but to surrender.

Hudson gave himself up after his lawyer negotiated a deal with a 'trusted' senior detective.

After two days of fruitless efforts to find him the breakthrough came when Northcote solicitor Patrick Dwyer contacted Detective Inspector Kim West, of the major crime investigation unit.

Hudson was frightened he would be intercepted and killed by police as he left his country hide-away to drive to a designated police station.

The first sign that Hudson had no alternative but to give himself up was when a Queensland lawyer who previously represented the suspect rang the homicide squad to say he could no longer act for him as it conflicted with the interests of his existing clients – the Hell's Angels.

The lawyer knew Hudson well. That's because Hudson had been involved in a vicious public gun battle in Queensland the previous year between the Finks and Hell's Angels gangs – but that time he was a victim.

He was shot in the jaw and back in the riot between bikies in the crowd at a kickboxing show at the Royal Pines Resort at Southport in March.

Three people were shot and two stabbed. Four were bikies, and the fifth was a teenager caught in the crossfire.

The fight was allegedly sparked by Hudson's defection from the Finks to the Hells Hell's Angels and by him encouraging others to follow.

The Angels recruited Hudson because of his links to local nightspots. He later moved to Sydney where he established new connections in the nightclub industry before he landed in Melbourne.

He had strong connections with bikie chapters in Queensland, Sydney, Adelaide and Melbourne but after the CBD shootings those links were severed.

Less than 48 hours after the shootings police were told the Hell's Angels had persuaded the suspect to give up. Whether the decision was a moral one based on what he was alleged to have done – or a practical one because the gang knew that while the suspect was at large they could expect to be the focus of an intense investigation – is largely irrelevant.

It was the right result.

Just after 4.30pm on June 20, Hudson was driven to the police station at Wallan, in Melbourne's north, from a safe house where he had been hiding.

He was unarmed and had suffered a badly damaged left wrist courtesy of a self-inflicted wound that would require plastic surgery.

Turning himself in means Hudson's fate will be decided under due process. Due process means an accused's guilt or innocence is decided by a jury selected from the broader community.

This suspect is perhaps lucky to have avoided judgement by his peers in the bikie world.

But the story of Christopher Wayne Hudson and his involvement in Melbourne nightclubs began six days before the CBD shooting, due to a meeting with a Collingwood footballer who was looking for adventure.

THE luckiest drunken footballer in Australia is not Alan Didak, whose close encounter with the Hell's Angels could have been life-threatening as well as career-ending, but his day-time opponent and night-time drinking mate, Melbourne's Colin Sylvia.

Even the sight of naked women dancing in the King Street strip club Spearmint Rhino was not enough to keep Sylvia awake.

Fatigued from a hard game of football on June 11, 2007, and

a harder night of drinking, he slowly descended into alcohol-induced unconsciousness.

Drunk and asleep, Sylvia was gently evicted by bouncers without incident. (A few days later he was quoted without a hint of irony as saying the mid-season break was an ideal opportunity to relax his mind and body.)

Without his football mate, Didak accepted a lift from Christopher Wayne Hudson, the man who would later stand accused of the Melbourne CBD shootings.

Didak's decision, the subsequent police investigation and the football club's initial farcical response, left many holes in the story that began as a drunken adventure and ended in allegations of gunfire.

For Melbourne and Collingwood, the Queen's Birthday match that day was the perfect punctuation mark for the mid-season break.

With no game scheduled the following week, the players had one of their few in-season opportunities to slip the AFL's tight lifestyle leash and head out on the town. But the idea of a few beers soon turned into a binge of mixed drinks and straight spirits as a group of players headed from nightclubs to strip clubs.

Eleven years earlier the previous Collingwood coach, Tony Shaw, banned his players from King Street bars, but that rule, like many others, had been quietly shelved.

After drinking at several venues, Melbourne and Collingwood stayers, including Didak and Sylvia, descended to the Bar 20 strip club.

While the other footballers drifted off, Didak and Sylvia tottered up King Street to Spearmint Rhino.

Drinking vodka, lime and sodas and straight shooters, they were flying by the early hours of Tuesday.

The last thing Didak needed was another drink but unwisely

he accepted one – this time a bourbon and cola – from a heavy-set man with burning eyes who said he was a fan of the Collingwood forward.

With Sylvia having lost interest and heading for the comfort of his bed, Didak chatted with the fan, who had recently moved from interstate.

The supporter, Christopher Hudson, followed two clubs. One was Collingwood and the second was the Hell's Angels.

But Didak's ability to judge the situation was severely affected by hours of drinking and he apparently saw no signs of danger from the man he had just met.

Some time after 3am, the two left, Didak slipping into the passenger side and Hudson behind the wheel of the bikie's powerful black Mercedes-Benz.

Didak would later tell police he had accepted an offer of a lift home to Kew when it all went horribly wrong. It is a version of events that detectives found harder to swallow than a free bourbon and Coke.

The football club's spin initially suggested Didak was a victim who wanted to head home but was virtually abducted and driven to the Hell's Angels East County headquarters in Campbellfield.

Supposedly terrified, he asked to be driven home, only to be embroiled in a shooting incident and a dangerous high-speed trip before being dropped in the city shaken – but not stirred enough to contact police.

'While in the car the person insisted that Alan accompany him to a bikie gang clubhouse. Alan felt he had no choice but to comply,' a poker-faced Collingwood chief executive Gary Pert told the media when the story finally broke after the CBD tragedy and Hudson's subsequent arrest.

Police suspect, but can't prove, that Hudson, 29, bragged that he was a Hell's Angel and invited Didak to the headquarters.

The footballer, curious to see inside the heavily fortified premises, accepted, an act that, while foolhardy, was not illegal.

It was only minutes after they left the strip club that Didak realised his night was going off the rails. Police allege that as the Mercedes sped over the Bolte Bridge, a high-powered handgun was produced and several shots were fired from the window.

Speeding along the Tullamarine Freeway, they arrived at the bikie headquarters around 4am.

Didak, 24, was greeted by at least one other member of the chapter. (Bikies rarely leave their headquarters vacant at any time to deter other gangs from raiding the property and police from breaking in to hide bugs.)

If Didak was terrified, he hid it well. When he was offered yet another drink, he accepted and stayed for up to 45 minutes before hopping back in the car, this time in the back seat of the coupe.

Two men sat in the front.

They sped off, flying through a red light across the Hume Highway just as a local police divisional van cruised past.

The police followed, but the Mercedes slipped into the Scania trucking industrial estate, out of sight, where it might have stayed if not spotted by an early-morning worker. It then cruised slowly out of the factory complex and stopped in Northbourne Road.

The police, having spotted the car, pulled up about 50 metres behind. Several shots allegedly were fired from the driver's side window of the Mercedes before it sped off again.

Police did not give chase. If they had, Didak might well have been permanently delisted, courtesy of a police bullet or a high-speed car crash.

Later police would find ten spent shells and one live one on the ground in two separate places on Northbourne Road –

meaning someone in the car fired a volley of shots before slipping into the estate and a second set when the police pulled up behind.

Because of the pressing danger of a gunman on Melbourne streets who was prepared to fire shots at police to avoid arrest, the investigation was immediately handed to the experts, the armed crime task force.

A police appeal that morning brought an immediate response through Crime Stoppers.

One caller reported a black Mercedes speeding wildly down the Tullamarine Freeway to Melbourne with one man in the back leaning forward and talking to the driver.

Detectives traced the Mercedes to a luxury vehicle dealer who at first denied any connection with Hudson. But detectives found the name of a Sydney woman who was alleged to have bought the car. She had once worked at Spearmint Rhino and knew Hudson.

Within 48 hours of the shooting police were looking for Hudson but they did not know where he was living and still did not have enough evidence to make an arrest.

Six days after the alleged shooting spree, Hudson is alleged to have opened fire in the city with tragic consequences.

The first police knew of a link between the footballer and the suspect was when they went to Hudson's apartment and found a handwritten note with Alan Didak's name and phone number.

A homicide detective and another from the armed task force quietly visited Didak away from the club to ask him some informal questions.

They gave him a few days to think deeply before he was to be formally interviewed.

But as rumours of Didak's involvement started to circulate in football-mad Melbourne, the interview was pushed forward, to be held discreetly at the Boroondara police station rather than at the St Kilda Road crime headquarters on June 28 – 10 days after the CBD shooting.

But the media were waiting. It was the lead item on TV news and made page one the following day. Didak gave police a version of events.

In some parts it was clear and in other parts strangely vague. He can remember the events at the strip club, the drive to the clubhouse, shots on the Bolte Bridge, drinks with the Hell's Angels and the dangerous trip back to the city. He can even remember leaning forward asking the driver to slow down on the freeway (an act independently corroborated by the Crime Stoppers call).

He was lucid enough when dropped at Flinders Street to even ask police in a passing van if they could give him a lift.

In the brief discussion he failed to mention his close encounter with the bikies.

The police declined the opportunity to act as an AFL shuttle service and Didak grabbed a cab.

Yet, when finally interviewed by detectives, Didak suffered a memory lapse that blanked out the crucial ten minutes when the shots were allegedly fired in the vicinity of police.

Perhaps he passed out – a convenient but entirely possible scenario considering the amount he had drunk.

No-one would really know whether Didak was asleep as Hudson isn't talking and the other passenger in the Mercedes is yet to be identified.

But what Didak did not know was there was another witness – not a person with a faulty memory, but a video camera.

When the driver of the Mercedes slipped into the Northbourne Road industrial estate to avoid police, a security camera filmed three men in the car, with the rear passenger conscious and clearly animated.

There is no doubt that after the event Didak was terrified. He feared the Hell's Angels, a group with a reputation of hunting down and silencing potential witnesses.

But Didak was safe. The Angels had turned on Hudson. He was on his own, whereas Didak had Collingwood.

Police briefed senior Collingwood officials on their investigation but were staggered when they saw how the player was initially portrayed as an innocent victim.

'He is not a suspect, he is not a victim, he is a witness and not a very good one,' a senior policeman said.

At the same time, police say suggestions that if Didak had come forward the CBD shooting may never have happened are unfair to the footballer, who on the known evidence was guilty only of being a fool and then remaining silent on the grounds of self-preservation.

But how silent? Police believe he did tell some team-mates, including those he was drinking with that night, what had happened after they had left.

Just hours after the Campbellfield incident he was on a plane to Queensland with the team. Collingwood staff hastily briefed club president Eddie McGuire as he was about to fly back to Australia from Europe.

But when he returned he quickly saw the club's position as untenable. Increasingly uncomfortable with what he saw as a less-than-comprehensive briefing, he shifted the position from victim Didak to last-chance Didak.

Far from Didak being an innocent caught up in events as first portrayed, McGuire now says, 'he was out too late, met bad people and it was just stupid'.

Later McGuire said Didak would have faced the sack if he had not shown remorse and that the footballer would only remain at the club if he accepted a nightclub and alcohol ban and a 1am curfew.

Meanwhile, Chief Commissioner Nixon provided some

unlikely support for Didak. 'I think it has been quite amazing to watch how he has been treated in the media. I think, as a young man, he's under enormous pressure and in some ways he's been damned without people really understanding what might be the circumstances,' she told 3AW.

Of course, the young police who were stopped in their tracks when shots were allegedly fired at them in Campbellfield would have also felt a touch of pressure before the Mercedes sped off.

At yet another Collingwood press conference, the slant that Didak was a victim was finally dumped.

With Eddie McGuire now in the driving seat, the player fronted the media to say his actions were 'reckless, embarrassing and stupid' and had damaged his reputation.

'I understand if I don't comply (with the restrictions) that is the end of my career at Collingwood,' he said.

Collingwood was worried its brand was being damaged. Its first Didak news conference was held with sponsors' logos visible. They were removed for subsequent briefings.

The Hell's Angels had a similar worry earlier in 2007 when they expelled a senior member. They solved the brand issue by removing the former member's Hell's Angels tattoos – with a steam iron.

AFTER he fired the shots that killed Brendan Keilar and wounded two others, the gunman placed the pistol barrel under his chin. For a moment, he seemed set to kill himself, but he lost his nerve and ran.

If he had pulled the trigger, it would have blown his head off. It's that sort of gun.

A court will formally decide who carried out the shootings but the handgun is already guilty. It is illegal in Australia on two counts: It combines a brutally heavy calibre with a short barrel that makes it easy to hide, a recipe for carnage in criminal hands, and it is a product of a sinister black market that, like the drug trade, ran out of control while authorities concentrated on easier targets.

'A highly concealable heavy hitter' is how one disgusted licensed gun dealer describes the weapon used to kill the heroic Melbourne lawyer, wound the equally brave Dutch backpacker and then injure an exotic dancer.

Overseas, such a pistol is used by 'narcotics agents, undercover cops and bodyguards', the dealer says. And gangsters, of course.

In Australia only an underworld enforcer or the dangerously deluded – or both – would carry such a man killer, more powerful than Victoria Police service revolvers. The pistol that blighted so many lives was found at a city building site soon after the shootings.

It was a .40 calibre Llama Minimax. It is small, relatively light and yet, with its hefty calibre, all too deadly.

Its stubby barrel is not made for accuracy – to hit targets or hunt – but to blow a hole in humans at murderously close range.

A few years ago, a handgun like that, or its Chinese equivalent, would have brought between $1000 and $2000. But the black market is so turbocharged by drugs, money and paranoia that it could bring much more now.

The word on the underworld rumour mill is that the city gunman paid $5000 for the murder weapon less than two weeks earlier.

For something that can destroy a life with such awful efficiency, the Llama is a relatively crude tool.

Not quite, perhaps, the 'gangster junk' that purists might label it, but so poorly thought of by legitimate target shooters that no dealership sells Llamas in Australia, and few were ever imported in the past.

The murder weapon almost certainly reached Australia through an underground network as pernicious as the drug trade – and inextricably entwined with it.

In the dog-eat-dog underworld, drug money and gun violence go together. Melbourne's underworld war proved that.

The path that ended with death in William Street began at a factory in northern Spain, the Basque region that has produced terrorism for decades and cheap pistols for much longer. For most of the twentieth century the area boasted three pistol-making plants, mostly making copies of American brands Colt and Smith & Wesson.

One factory, run by the Gabilondo Y Cia company, made pistols at Vitoria until 2003, when it moved to Legutiano under a new name, Fabrinor.

Arms dealers sell to whoever buys. In 1943, the firm supplied the Nazis in German-occupied territories with thousands of specially badged pistols.

After the war it found new markets, including a niche for a two-shot 'pistol' disguised as an office stapler, which authorities feared would be used by terrorists.

From the mid-1990s until it closed in 2005 the firm was making 20,000 pistols a year, with 17,000 a year going to the gun-hungry US.

It is almost certainly one of these that shot Brendan Keilar and the other two victims in Melbourne.

So how did it get here? While it's possible the pistol was exported to the Philippines and then smuggled here by light plane or small boats through Papua New Guinea, Timor or the Pacific Islands, it is far more likely it came via America.

It was probably bought there as part of a job lot for as little as $US400 ($A470) new or even $US200 second-hand. And it's likely the buyer was fronting for an outlaw bikie gang with a proven smuggling route all fixed.

**Don Hancock: Former Western Australia police crime chief, killed in bikie bombing after a mystery shooting on the goldfields.**

**Every dog has its day: Carl Williams in happier times, when he gave the press conferences and the police said 'no comment'. It didn't last.**

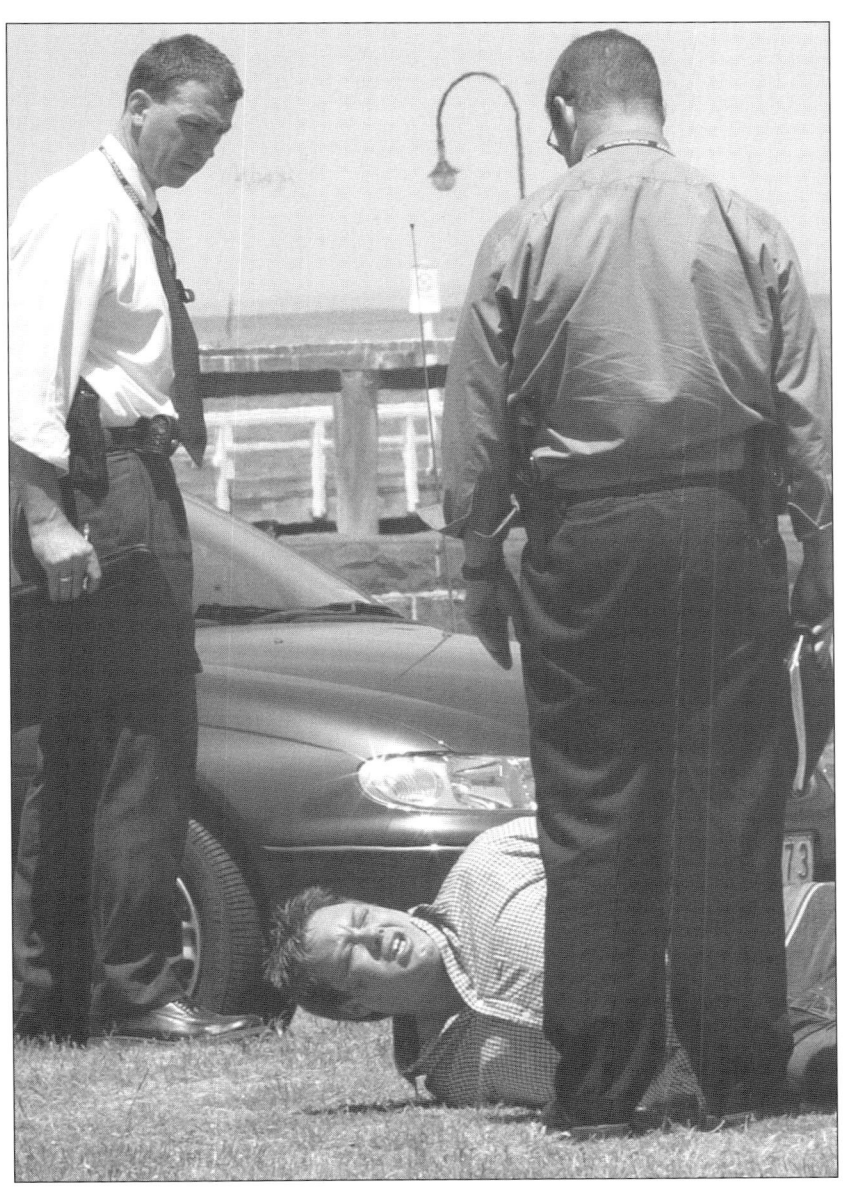

**Cop this: The day the man behind the gangland killings found the tide had turned against him.**

**Purana task force members led by dogged detective inspector Gavan Ryan (centre) just after Williams had been sentenced to 35 years. This time, police held the press conference.**

**Too late for shoosh: Carl Williams' fiercely loyal mother Barb with the drug dealer's then latest glamour puss. Maybe the girl was just wagging school.**

What's the story? Carl Williams is a fat drug dealer who won't be out of jail before he's 71, if he lives that long. Yet this young woman turned up at court daily to support him. Go figure.

**Black widow: An angry Judy Moran rolls into court in boutique mourning clothes to see Carl Williams sentenced. Her late son Jason had put holes in his manners, and Williams's belly, with a .22 pistol.**

Unhappy: Roberta Williams (far right, in the cap) expresses her displeasure to her chubby hubby's new buxom best friend.

**You've got to be kidding (1): What could be the last photograph of Carl Williams, taken in court moments before Justice Betty King sentenced him to a minimum 35 years jail. He stopped smiling then.**

You've got to be
kidding (2): Ben
Cousins' bizarre
statement to camera in
which he admitted but
failed to explain his
involvement with
drugs, at the same
time wearing a
garment rejected by
*Miami Vice*. Go figure.

**Rehab West Coast style: Ben Cousins with unidentified female who may or may not be a drug counsellor.**

**Collingwood footballer Alan Didak on a different type of bike. He lived to regret his night out with a Hells Angel.**

**I'm no Angel: Alan Didak faces the media to speak about his drunken adventures with outlaw bikie gang members. His memory was shaky.**

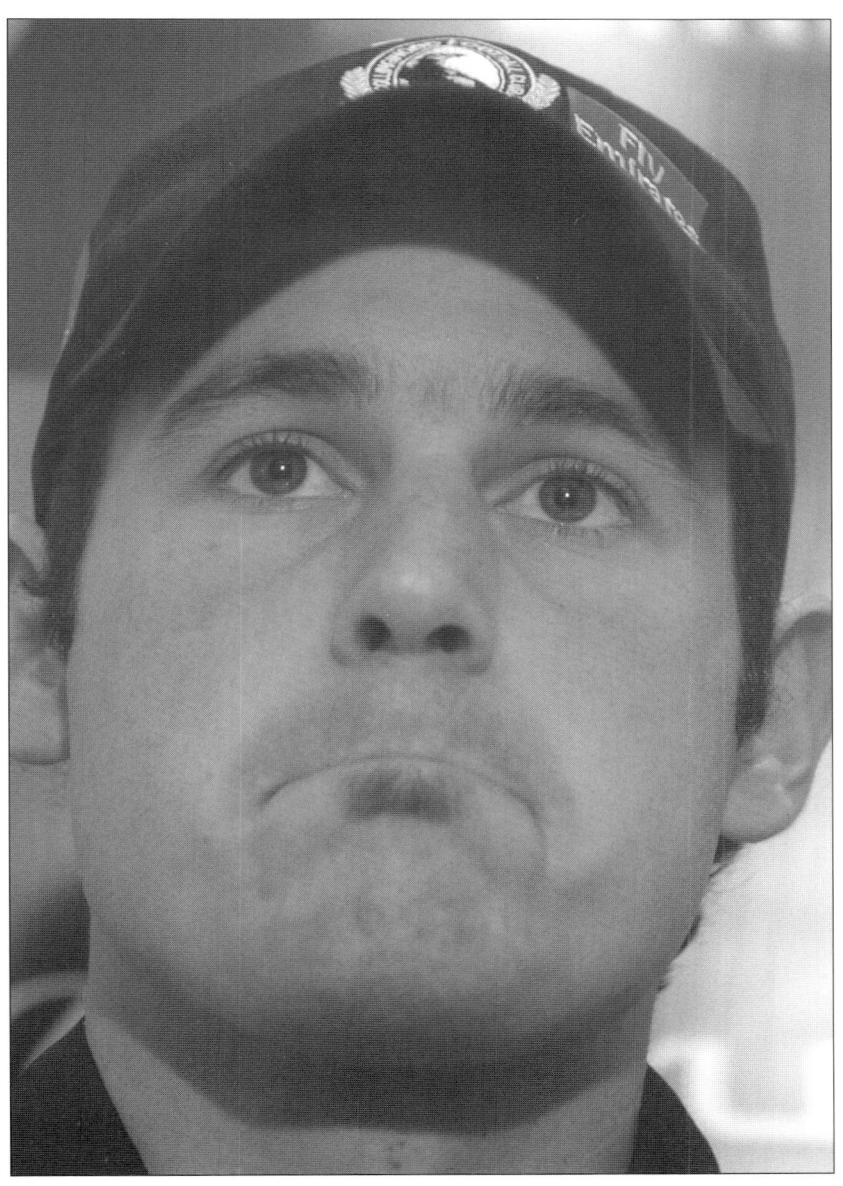

**Didak searches his memory. Only two things are known: Shots were fired, and there were holes in his story.**

Hudson after his arrest: Gave himself up after gentle
persuasion from Hells Angels.

Christopher
Wayne Hudson:
Alleged CBD
killer, former
Fink and Hells
Angel gang
member, keen
Collingwood
supporter.

Outlaw bikies are known for trafficking amphetamines. But their link with guns goes back further and runs deeper.

When police raid bikie gangs looking for drugs they do not always find them, but they usually find firearms.

Such as in the raid on a Nomads clubhouse in suburban Thomastown in 2004 when a policeman accidentally kicked a step, which fell apart to reveal five handguns.

Another raid, in country Victoria, uncovered a cannon, two machine-guns and night-vision goggles at a bikie house.

From their beginnings in the US after World War II, the 'one percenter' outlaw gangs fostered an image of hard-living 'cowboys' riding steel horses across a mythical frontier, guns on hips.

A lot of rebel gang members were ex-military people who knew too much about guns to live without them. Next step was to trade in them, and so gunrunning has also always been a bikie cash cow.

Australian Hell's Angels brought back the original recipe for amphetamines from the US in the 1970s and bikies have controlled a slice of the Australian 'speed' since.

But guns, the other side of their business, still have to be imported.

According to underworld sources and former police, the most common smuggling method is to hide pistols in engine blocks and mechanical parts imported from the US.

'Bikies are constantly involved with cars and trucks. They loved bringing in big cars like Cadillacs to restore and drive around,' says a former drug squad policeman.

'They would fill the sump with stripped-down pistols.' Sniffer dogs don't find guns covered in oil. And, hidden in engine blocks, they are undetected by X-rays. The only way to find them would be to intercept and strip every engine passing through every port.

Barely one in twenty shipping containers is searched, so that's unlikely.

Even if systematic searches were done at big ports such as Melbourne and Sydney, officials might not be as efficient at some smaller ports around Australia. Such as in Tasmania. Not just Hobart but sleepy Burnie and Devonport.

Underworld lore has it that most new black market pistols arrive in Melbourne from the south, across Bass Strait.

If 'the Territory' is the Deep North, Tasmania is the Deep South. Before the Port Arthur massacre in 1996, Tasmania was one of four states and territories with much laxer gun laws – and enforcement – than in more heavily populated Victoria and NSW.

A sparse population scattered over a large area of wilderness, a tradition of hunting and fishing and a rural-based economy meant it had more in common with outback Queensland or the Northern Territory than with Victoria.

Gun use there reflected that – at all levels of society. In a place where many people are related or connected, gun enthusiasts include police, and prison and Customs officers as well as farmers, fishermen and forestry workers, some of whom resented the post-Port Arthur laws that demanded they hand in certain weapons.

Not all did, hiding guns and creating a cache of 'orphan' (unregistered) guns that became part of a black market linking some former mainstream shooters with underworld elements.

Enter the bikies. Tasmania offers cheap land in isolated areas, yet is only a short plane trip or boat ride from Melbourne.

Inevitably bikie gangs such as the Coffin Cheaters and the Black Uhlans saw it as a good place to do things away from prying eyes.

Rural solitude is ideal for producing amphetamines and dealing in cannabis and guns. With the state's small population, low employment and depressed wages, the bikies and their associates exert influence with both muscle and money.

It is widely known in underworld and police circles that large groups of bikies ride the *Spirit of Tasmania* back and forth regularly, and not to take the fresh air.

Vehicles and luggage are not routinely searched and, in any case, the bikies are skilled hands at building caches for drugs and guns into vehicles.

In theory, guns should be no easier to import to Tasmania's ports than those on the mainland. Anecdotally, they are. One reason is that until the 2001 terrorist attacks, US Navy ships regularly called into Hobart (and Fremantle) en route to the Middle East.

Authorities either deny or ignore it for diplomatic reasons, but it is a fact that US sailors routinely smuggled in large numbers of handguns, easily done because the sailors do not have to clear Customs.

There is proof this also happened in Melbourne, and every reason to think it still happens in any port where US warships call for rest and recreation.

On November 12, 1998, for instance, the huge aircraft carrier USS Abraham Lincoln anchored in the Derwent River and most of its 5500 sailors came ashore over five days.

One group carried a wooden crate through the rudimentary 'beach guard' on Princes Wharf, hailed a taxi and went to a nightclub for a pre-arranged meeting.

Inside the crate were 40 new Colt .45 calibre semi-automatic pistols, a favourite US military sidearm. Not only lethal handguns, these were prized collectors' items commanding a premium that made the crate of 40 worth more than $100,000 on the black market.

Today, they would be worth up to three times as much, an indication of how the black market has been inflated by drug money, and the alarming penchant of nightclub poseurs to carry 'a piece'.

Although smuggling guns is an easy way for American sailors (and soldiers) to raise local currency, the aircraft carrier crew was not after money this time.

As part of a pre-arranged plan, it swapped the crate of pistols for another crate.

This held a breeding pair of young Tasmanian devils, trapped to order a few days before near Richmond, east of Hobart.

Americans are fascinated by the animals because of the popularity of the Warner Bros cartoon character Taz. The devils were smuggled on board the ship.

And the pistols? Almost all of them were taken to the mainland and sold covertly, not all to active criminals.

A former policeman, posted to the Melbourne docks to protect US ships from anti-nuclear protesters in the mid-1980s, recalls several of his colleagues swapping their police jackets for new pistols taken from the ship's armoury.

'The first time I went was for the USS *Sterett*. For some reason the crew were mad on collecting jackets everywhere they went. Obviously the armoury officer had done a deal with the sailors, because they would take your jacket, then direct you to the armoury guy and he would give you the pistol,' the former policeman said.

'The funny thing was that every time a (US) warship came into port after that, cops would be running around collecting jackets to swap for pistols.

'They must have got dozens. From memory they were nine-millimetre Berettas.'

US Navy ships have visited Australian ports only rarely since September 11, 2001.

But plenty of cruise ships and freighters visit, and dozens of them visit Tasmania's ports. Somehow, somewhere, illegal handguns are flowing in unchecked, according to underworld and police sources.

In Melbourne's northern suburbs, underground dealers have boxes full of American-made handguns: Colts, Rugers and Smith & Wessons, in calibres from .22 to .45.

Most sell for about $5000 each, but $20,000 will get five, allowing a cashed-up buyer to sell four to others and keep one 'for nothing'. Those willing to take the risk can drive them to Sydney, where they bring up to $8000 each.

Handguns have become a fashion accessory for even low level drug dealers who want the gangster lifestyle centred on money, sex and violence.

The most favoured pistols are the most concealable: like the lives of most of those who buy them, they are nasty, brutish and short.

And every one that ends up on the streets, under a car seat or stuck down the back of someone's jeans is only a heartbeat away from repeating the horror of what happened in Melbourne in June 2007.

# CHAPTER 5

# Where there's smoke

'The gun's here in our yard.
The rotten mongrel has hidden it here.'

THEY stayed sealed in a police plastic evidence bag for more than twenty years. The sort of incidental material gathered at every murder scene – just in case.

Three damp cigarette butts found near some shrubs and trees at a mullock heap ... where a sniper waited for his target to arrive around midnight on April 15, 1985.

The shot of 44 metres was an easy one for an experienced shooter – armed with the high-powered rifle steadied on the fork of a small tree just 250mm from the damp ground.

The killer lay on his stomach, making him virtually invisible. Not that the men on the other side of the deserted county road would have bothered to look.

They weren't soldiers on patrol or gangsters in the middle of drug deal. They were four transport workers loading a truck for the nightly midnight run to Mildura.

The depot was floodlit with powerful fluorescent lights – meaning anyone could look in, while those inside could not focus on anything hidden in the darkness. But what had appeared an easy shot in planning became less straightforward in practice.

Firstly the driver of the truck backed into the depot at a slight angle, leaving the sniper's view momentarily blocked.

Then when the truckie jumped out of the cab he quickly went inside, swinging open both rear doors of his truck, again blocking the view.

The gunman moved about three metres to the left for a clean shot and waited silently while the driver helped load the boxes from McPhee Transport Depot in Bellevue Road, Bendigo.

It took only minutes to load, but time was everything in this cut-throat business. The driver had already picked up mail two blocks away at the Australia Post depot and would head straight off to pick up freight from a late Ansett truck delivery before driving hours through the night to Mildura.

Kevin Pearce, a hardworking battler who tried many jobs before moving into the freelance courier world, shut the doors of his van and stood momentarily in the light as McPhee's night manager Paul Thompson handed him an envelope with his payment.

It took only a few seconds but it was enough.

The sniper fired just one shot from his powerful .308 hunting rifle. It struck Pearce on the left side, leaving a gaping wound that his shocked mates tried to staunch with a toilet roll. A sliver of the bullet damaged his spinal cord so badly he would have been left a paraplegic. If he had lived.

Kevin Hugh Pearce, father of three daughters, lingered for three weeks before he died.

Within minutes of the shooting those close to the victim believed they knew who was behind the attack.

But two decades later, the only suspect remains free and apparently unaffected by the whispers that continue today. The case looked like remaining one of many in which police claim to know who did it but lack the solid evidence to convict. So when in 2006 detectives sent the three John Player Special Virginia 25s cigarette butts found at the scene for DNA examination they did so as a matter of routine rather than in hope of a late breakthrough.

The results, however, were anything but routine and were positive enough to breathe new life into an old case.

KEVIN Pearce, 45, was a hard worker determined to remain his own boss. He and his wife, Joan, ran milk bars and guesthouses before moving into the dog-eat-dog transport business.

The work was tough and margins slender for owner–drivers so in 1982 Pearce joined forces with two others, Bill Matthews and Barry Coates, to form CMP (Coates, Matthews, Pearce) Trucking Contractors to carry freight and mail to northern Victoria.

With eight large trucks and two vans they planned to become the major transport firm in Bendigo. At the heart of the business were the Australia Post mail runs that provided regular income and allowed the partners to load their trucks with private contract work to make a profit.

Pearce controlled the Mildura (valued at $61,000) and Echuca ($49,000) mail runs while Matthews kept the Robinvale contract. Matthews was a ruthless self-made man whose reputation for being keen on a dollar was matched by his reluctance to spend one.

Some of his associates claimed his paperwork was sloppy and when there was an error in accounts it would invariably fall in his favour. And the tough truckie rarely seemed bothered when those errors were revealed.

Some of those burnt by Matthews vowed to never again deal with him but working for a bad boss was better than not working at all so many returned.

But from the beginning the CMP partners argued and after a year Coates bailed out.

Pearce was uncomfortable when Matthews employed his mistress, Dianne Robertson, as the office manager – believing they were not making enough money to employ her.

According to Joan Pearce, Matthews did the books and was always short of money for accounts forcing the Pearces to use $5000 from their milk bar to top up the trucking firm.

Tired of excuses over shortfalls the Pearces left the partnership in February 1984 and commissioned a local solicitor to recover the money they claimed they were owed. Matthews was also committed for trial on a charge of stealing 10,000 litres of fuel from the company. And Pearce was to be a witness against him.

The one-time partners became ferocious competitors and Pearce began to win work from Matthews, who made it clear he would use any means to fight back.

'After the partnership broke up Kevin used to give me the impression that he was frightened of what Matthews might do to him. I think Kevin was also scared for the whole family, not just for himself,' Mrs Pearce said.

'I know Kevin used to be petrified about going to pick the freight up but I did not know exactly why.'

The breaking point appeared to be when Pearce was awarded a contract from McPhee Transport to deliver freight to Mildura. Matthews was furious, as he had been confident he would win the tender.

Pearce's oldest daughter told police, 'In about January 1985 McPhee's Transport contacted Dad and offered them their delivery run to Mildura, which Bill Matthews had previously had.

Dad accepted this offer and took the contract from Bill Matthews.

'Dad told me after Christmas this year that he had been told by someone at the Bendigo Mail Centre that Bill Matthews said he was going to get him. Dad has been worried that Matthews would get him and Dad actually said he thought Matthews would shoot him.'

If the third partner Barry John Coates thought when he quit the company that he could walk away from the conflict he was soon to learn there was no way out.

Even when he was in the firm he found someone was holding a grudge. According to his wife, Dianne, Coates found the truck he drove was repeatedly vandalised, leaving brake lines and the radiator hose cut.

Like many who dealt with Matthews, Coates decided to quit while he was behind believing he had been ripped off for thousands of dollars.

But when Matthews later wanted his former partner to help out with the trucks Coates decided practicality outweighed principle.

'Barry wanted to keep on the good side of him instead of the bad side of him,' his wife explained.

Enraged by losing business Matthews escalated the commercial war. 'Bill started to send his own truck to Mildura at a loss, just (to) be vindictive,' Mrs Coates said.

'I know Bill wanted the Mildura run desperately. I think Bill wanted to buy Kevin out but Kevin refused.'

According to Mrs Coates, Matthews believed if Pearce was out of the way he would inherit the Mildura run. 'I heard from Barry that Bill was going to shoot Kevin to get him out of the road ... Barry tried to talk him out of it and told him that he should not be a fool.'

It is clear that Barry Coates took Matthews' threats seriously. So seriously he told his daughter, Sharon, while at their Sealake caravan, 'Nobody wants to get in Billy Matthews' way.'

'Dad said someone was going to get hurt. He didn't say who was going to get hurt, he just said Billy Matthews was going to do the hurting.'

It was April 13, 1985.

Two days later, an unknown sniper shot Kevin Pearce.

When local police and later homicide detectives began to investigate the shooting of Pearce it became clear that Matthews was the prime suspect.

He hated the victim, was in the vicinity, had made threats and believed he would profit from the death.

But when police began to interview potential witnesses they found some varied from vague to deliberately uncooperative.

Few wanted to stand up to Bill Matthews.

One had good reason to be worried. Just days after the shooting Matthews' lover, Dianne Robertson, drove to the Coates' house in Adams Street, Bendigo to tell them a rifle was hidden in their backyard.

Coates looked around an old van body used for storage and found the rifle hidden under a wheel arch with a plastic bag containing a gun magazine and ammunition.

Coates went inside and told his wife, who was preparing dinner, 'The gun's here in our yard. The rotten mongrel has hidden it here.'

He told her he planned to dump the rifle, even though he thought the gun was used to shoot his former business partner. 'I just didn't want to get involved. We got rid of the rifle and we just wanted to forget it,' she said.

Dianne Coates told police they talked for hours about what to do with the gun, briefly entertaining the thought of going to the police before deciding to stay silent – for one overpowering reason – fear.

'Barry was scared of Bill and getting shot.'

The couple drove to Lake Eppalock where he threw the gun

into the spot known as the Metcalf Pool. If he suffered guilt pangs for his involvement in the cover-up he hid it well. He continued to drive for Matthews even though he was convinced his former partner shot Pearce.

The gun would have remained hidden if someone with a conscience had not come forward. A woman rang police and told them Matthews shot Pearce then hid the gun in Barry Coates' backyard.

She claimed Matthews threatened the Coates family and Coates and his wife then dumped the gun near Lake Eppalock. The caller was Sharon Coates, Barry's daughter.

When confronted by police Coates promised to co-operate, taking them to the lake where he waded in to recover the weapon.

But Coates remained a frightened man and initially refused to implicate the suspect further. While the truckie remained at best a reluctant witness his wife and daughter were more forthcoming.

Sharon told police that straight after the sniper attack 'Billy Matthews told him (Coates) over the phone that he had shot Pearcey. Dad has told me that Billy Matthews has told him if he says anything about the shooting, about any of it, then Dad would be next. Dad is very scared of Billy Matthews.'

Coates' version of the call was less colourful and he refused to directly implicate the red-hot suspect. If Coates had stood up and made a statement that Matthews had admitted the shooting it would have been enough to lay a murder charge. But he didn't.

He remembered a call that night that woke him from a deep sleep. 'I have a vague recollection of Bill Matthews ringing me at home … I seem to remember him telling me that Pearce had been shot.'

According to Mrs Coates a few days after the gun was

dumped Matthews asked if they could recover the rifle, 'because he might need it again. Barry was scared but he told him it was gone for good'.

Later, according to Mrs Coates, Matthews told her husband, 'I know I can do it now mate'.

Sharon Coates went further, telling police Matthews had confessed to her father. She said her step-mother said Matthews told Coates, 'I'm in the big league now, I'm a murderer … Billy Matthews laughed as he said it.'

She said her father told her, 'Billy Matthews shot Pearcey because Pearcey's trod on too many toes, mainly Matthews.'

After talking to Sharon Coates police decided to have another chat to Barry showing him the statements from his wife and daughter. At first Coates tried to blame a faulty memory for withholding vital evidence. 'I'm not sure I said those things or not. I'm not saying that what they say is wrong. I just can't remember saying these things.'

He opened the possibility Matthews paid a hitman to kill his commercial rival. 'I am pretty sure that Bill Matthews spoke to me of hiring somebody to get rid of Pearce. I can't remember when he said this before Pearce's death. It would have been a long time before.'

The gun recovered from the lake was a .308 Valmet Rifle, loaded with Musgrove K 6 ammunition with one in the breech. It was the same ammunition and the same calibre used to kill Pearce. Police were confident that having linked the recovered murder weapon to the suspect they had made their case against Matthews.

But firearm tests showed the gun from the lake was not the one used to kill Pearce.

Police traced the history of the rifle. It was stolen from a transport depot in Footscray from the same loading bay where Matthews picked up freight for his Bendigo run. Police now knew he was a thief but they still couldn't prove he was a murderer.

WHY were people so quick to believe that Matthews would kill his partner? It would seem the hard-headed truckie revelled in a tough-guy image and gave the impression he could organise the shooting of anyone who stood in his way.

Pearce's nephew Clement Pearce said that at a party his uncle told him Matthews was out to get him because he was a witness in the petrol theft case and was trying to recover $30,000.

'Kevin told me at a party that there was a bullet in the spout for him. He said Matthews would point the gun but wouldn't pull the trigger ... I know that Kevin was very scared of what Matthews would do to him.'

Clement Pearce knew his uncle had reasons to be wary. Four years earlier Matthews was running illegal gaming cards in Bendigo and wanted to scare off a rival. Clement Pearce told police Matthews tried to enlist him to recruit heavies from Melbourne to solve the problem.

The younger Pearce, who drank in a few rough Melbourne pubs, responded, 'I'll see if I can arrange someone'.

At first Pearce thought it was just beer bravado but a week later Matthews followed up with a call allegedly saying, 'I just want them to give them a hiding. If that doesn't work, if we have to shoot them we'll shoot them'.

'Matthews had said to me that he could get someone from Bendigo to do it, but it was too close to home.'

Clement waited a respectable time, then rang to say he couldn't help.

Motor mechanic Emmanuel Schembri was another dragged into the increasingly bitter trucking conflict. He said Pearce told him Matthews owed him $32,000 and he was worried he would never get it back.

'Kevin was scared of Bill and would never drive past Bill's depot which was around the corner from Kevin's depot. Kevin also told me he didn't trust Bill and thought that Bill would shoot him.'

Schembri told police, 'Bill told me that if he wanted to get someone bad enough, he would ring up and send someone down and he would be shot. He also told me that he would alibi himself by being a couple of hundred miles away. I think Dianne, his secretary, was there at the time.'

Later in evidence at the Coroner's Court Schembri's memory began to play tricks and he was no longer '100 percent sure Matthews had used the word shot'.

'I wish I never sort of said anything about that shooting because it could've just been a passing conversation, you know, between two blokes.'

While many of those close to the men seemed to suffer unexplained bouts of amnesia someone was trying to help police. They received an anonymous tip-off that a yellow car was seen leaving the scene of the crime. The same colour car as that owned by Dianne Robertson.

As a policeman, Roger Irwin was used to being an informal problem solver for friends and family. But when Kevin Pearce began to talk to him at a family party in Broadmeadows on January 12, 1985 the detective knew this was deadly serious.

'He appeared very worried and said there was a person in Bendigo that was out to get him.' He said his ex-business partner 'had a bullet in the gun for him'.

He said Pearce confided, 'He threatened to shoot me a couple of times.'

Irwin told him to notify Bendigo detectives about the threats and gave him his home number to ring if there were further problems.

Maxwell Yates was a truckie who had worked for both

Matthews and Pearce. He was rung on the night of the shooting and drove straight to McPhee's. Just before the victim was loaded into the ambulance he was still worried about the nightly run, telling Yates to 'Take the truck and do Mildura.'

Yates told the dying man he would look after everything and then asked, 'Who mate, Matthews?'

Kevin nodded his head as if to say yes.


BILL Matthews is a straight talker as well as allegedly a straight shooter. When interviewed by police he did not conceal his hatred of Pearce.

'Personally I think he's an arrogant fat c... and he doesn't want to work. That's my personal opinion of the bloke and ... that's not why we had the argument. The partnership broke up. The reason was I didn't think he was working as hard as I was and I said, "Look, you go your way and I'll go mine".'

'I haven't had any contact with the guy for twelve months.'

'I don't really give a fuck about him as I said, I feel sorry for his missus and kids because none of them have screwed up.'

He said that on the night of the shooting he drove to Melbourne with his de facto wife, Keryn Strawhorn, to pick up and deliver freight, dropping her at their Bendigo home shortly after 11pm. He then took the truck to his shed in Adams Street where two men helped load goods until 1am. Around 3.35am he left the shed to drive his Isuzu van to his brother-in-law's house then walked the two blocks home.

His alibi witnesses were the two men who were in the shed with him until 1am, meaning Matthews could not have slipped away around midnight to kill his enemy.

But the men did leave the shed to pick up mail freight just before midnight and did not return for more than 30 minutes – giving him the window of opportunity to get to the mullock heap and return without being seen.

His depot was just two minutes by car from the mullock heap. Police later tracked footprints from where the sniper fired the shot over two small hills to a reserve where the getaway car must have been parked.

They noted the killer slipped several times clambering over one of the hills and used his rifle as a crutch to struggle over the sandy rise.

There was another person in the shed that night with Bill Matthews – his loyal and loving assistant, Dianne Robertson, who was prepared to work until nearly 4am alone with her boss.

Shortly after Pearce died Matthews asked a friend to enquire if he could buy the dead man's trucks – 'only to sort of help Joan out'.

In June 1986 Coroner Hal Hallenstein held an inquest into the death and under the law at the time it was a committal hearing to see if Matthews should stand trial for murder.

Matthews and Robertson did not give evidence on the grounds of self-incrimination, nor did Barry and Dianne Coates.

Hallenstein found, 'One would have to conclude that ... it (the murder) was carried out by a person who had some knowledge of Mr Pearce's routine.

'It was a well-planned and clearly calculated operation.'

'My formal findings on this matter are that Kevin Hugh Pearce ... was shot by or by the arrangement and organisation of William James Matthews.'

Matthews was committed for trial but the Director of Public Prosecutions reviewed the case and the charges were withdrawn.

As he was never acquitted before a jury the charges can be reissued if fresh evidence is uncovered.

He did stand trial for allegedly stealing fuel from the company. But with Pearce dead the theft charge against

Matthews was terminally damaged and he was acquitted in the County Court.

Twenty-two years after the shooting Bill Matthews still runs a flourishing trucking firm in Bendigo. He works sixteen hours a day, has more than $300,000 in the bank and his one social outlet is the Essendon Football Club.

Police still don't know if Matthews fired the fatal shot or hired someone to kill his business rival.

These days he does not feel inclined to discuss the death of his former partner. 'I don't wish to say anything. I received legal advice not to make any comments and I don't think I should go against that now. I hope you understand, thank you.'

Kevin Pearce's daughter, Donna said, 'Our Dad was a loving, caring person with strong, honest values.

'He was a law-abiding man who always put his family first and taught us right from wrong. We are extremely proud to be the daughters of Kevin and Joan Pearce.

'Our lives were shattered 22 years ago when Dad was callously shot and we watched him suffer and die over three long weeks. Our father was a hardworking man who was just too trusting.

'We plead with anyone with information to please contact police.'

The head of the re-investigation, Acting Detective Sergeant Tim Argall, said 'Kevin Pearce was a hardworking man who was just trying to earn an honest living.'

'We have established there are several people who know what happened in the lead-up to the shooting, the events that happened that night and the immediate aftermath.'

'I think there would be people whose consciences would still bother them even after more than twenty years. They know who did it and they have to live with it.'

He said the case was still open. 'Murder never goes away.'

When detectives from the cold case unit received the DNA result from the three cigarette butts (found where the sniper waited) they were not expecting a breakthrough, as Matthews did not smoke.

But his lover and alibi witness did.

The butts were from Dianne Robertson.

One puzzle remains. If the killer smoked the cigarettes, why were three butts found at the scene and a packet with only one missing left neatly on a rock?

Were they planted to push the finger of suspicion away from the non-smoking Matthews? Only one man knows and he's not talking.

# CHAPTER 6

# Peter Dupas: the predator

'It was his eyes, they were blank. There was something peculiar about him. He was evil-looking.'

THE little girl was so small she had to clamber on a grave to clean the top of the headstone of her grandfather's tomb in Melbourne's sprawling Fawkner Cemetery.

The grave was taller than most in the Roman Catholic section so the ten-year-old was perched above the thousands of concrete and marble memorials that surrounded her.

She was in the perfect position to pick up any sound in the near-silence of the cemetery while her mother, who was bending to place flowers on the grave, remained surrounded by the tall tombstones.

Perhaps that is why Lisa Tinker heard something that her mother didn't. Or maybe it is that young ears and uncluttered minds pick up what adults can't. But now, more than eight years later, she knows what she heard.

It was a scream. 'I can still recall this scream in my mind. I can recall this scream because it sounded frightening and that's why it has stuck with me.'

She said to her mother, 'Did you hear that scream?' But Maria, who wanted to visit other family graves and be home by 5pm, did not want to be distracted. She checked her watch to see if they were running late and saw that it was just before 4pm. She then told her daughter, 'Don't worry about it, just hurry up and clean the grave.'

But Lisa Tinker did worry about it and so did the whole family when they saw on television the next day that a young woman had been murdered in the cemetery.

I heard that girl scream,' she reminded her mother, who didn't need reminding.

That night her father rang Crime Stoppers with the information.

It was one of thousands of tips and tiny pieces of information handed to police over the next eight years as part of the complex investigation into the murder of Mersina Halvagis, 25, who was stabbed to death as she tended her grandmother's grave on November 1, 1997.

It was just one snippet but in a police re-investigation in 2005 it became part of a mosaic of hundreds of fragments of information that points to one man – a predator who chooses to remain silent and refuses to answer questions about the case.

Much of the information was available soon after the murder but some key witnesses also chose to remain silent – not wanting to become involved – until years later they felt compelled to make the calls to police that helped breathe new life into the old case.

Mersina's father, George, has devoted his life to finding his daughter's killer. He has lobbied politicians, held vigils, handed out flyers, haunted courts and prodded police.

'All I have ever wanted was the truth,' Mr Halvagis says.

Mersina's sister, Dimitria, told a victims' conference late in 2005 how it was impossible to move on and how she suffered flashbacks to the recurring image of Mersina desperately fighting for her life.

The reward for information into the murder began at $50,000, was raised to $100,000 and was finally increased to $1 million.

The homicide squad initially investigated the case, before it was transferred to a task force. Then in 2005, in one last effort, all information was again re-analysed by Senior Detective Paul Scarlett.

While the case remains complex, the conclusion is remarkably simple.

More than 100 names have been nominated to police as the killer. All but one has been eliminated.

Detectives are convinced that Peter Norris Dupas – a man who has already twice been sentenced to life for the murders of Margaret Maher and Nicole Patterson – killed Mersina Halvagis.

They believe that Dupas, who has attacked women throughout Victoria for 31 years, has killed at least six times – Helen McMahon (February 1985), Renita Brunton (November 1993), Margaret Maher (October 1997), Mersina Halvagis (November 1997), Kathleen Downes (December 1997) and Nicole Patterson (April 1999).

They also know the serial killer will never confess. At least to them.

MERSINA Halvagis's boyfriend, Angelo Gorgievski, was feeling lazy that Saturday morning and wanted to take a sickie from his job at the Epping branch of Target. But Mersina, who had stayed the previous night at Gorgievski's parents' home in Mill Park, came from a family with a strict work ethic and she wouldn't hear of it. 'I told her I didn't want to go to work but she forced me to go.'

The couple had been going out for five years after they first met at the La Trobe University ball in 1992. They'd recently become engaged and bought a block of land in Mill Park where they planned to build their first home.

They had just come through a bad patch when the pressure of wedding arrangements had made them quarrel, but they had decided to relax and, according to Gorgievski, were planning to move in together within weeks.

Once his fiancée persuaded him to go to work, she said she would take the train home to Mentone, but Gorgievski told her to take his car.

She then said she would visit her grandmother's grave at Fawkner Cemetery on the way home. Later she planned to return to her boyfriend's parents' home for dinner.

When All Saints Day falls on a weekend, cemeteries receive more than their usual number of visitors, so it was a busy day for the Fawkner Cemetery Tea Room catering manager Elva Hayden.

But she was able to remember the polite young woman who asked for a bunch of the long-stemmed blue and white statice flowers and then, as an afterthought, two bottles of Sprite lemonade.

A check of the cash register roll showed the $9.70 sale was made at 3.47pm. The purchaser was Mersina Halvagis.

She drove her boyfriend's red Telstar TX5 to a small car park at the Greek Orthodox section of the cemetery then walked about 50 metres and passed 32 graves before reaching the dark grey headstone where her grandmother, Mersina, had been buried the previous year.

On her regular visits she had left flowers on the neglected graves of strangers, hating the thought of anyone being forgotten, but this time she walked straight along the gravel path to the grave without stopping.

Police profilers say the killer probably established a beat and wandered the cemetery for days or weeks looking for the right moment to strike.

He probably went through dry runs, following other women, but chose not to attack, either because he was disturbed or because he was rehearsing his plans until he was ready.

A police reconstruction indicates Mersina was bending over the grave, probably placing the flowers in a vase when she was attacked from behind. She turned and was likely to have been blinded by the sun as she fought for her life. She was struck viciously to the head but although she was tiny – just 155 centimetres and less than 50 kilograms – she continued to fight and scream for help.

Her attacker had a knife and stabbed her repeatedly. Her body was later found in an empty plot three graves from where her grandmother was buried.

Her shoes were either placed or thrown near her so a casual observer who glanced up the path would not have seen anything out of the ordinary.

The killer, who must have been covered in blood, managed to slip out of the cemetery unnoticed using a planned escape route.

When Mersina Halvagis did not return to Mill Park she was reported missing. Her boyfriend tried to retrace her steps, driving from his house to the cemetery and then to the Halvagis's Mentone home. Eventually he jumped the cemetery fence and found his car. When police arrived, they discovered her body around 4.35am.

An autopsy showed the extent of the injuries. She had a two centimetre wound on the right side of the forehead above the eye. She had been stabbed from the knees to the neck but most of the wounds were concentrated around the breast area.

The wounds were deep and inflicted with great force with a sharp knife. Her top had been pulled over her head onto her chest and two belt loops on her pants broken in the struggle.

UNDERBELLY 11

NO-ONE can find a pivotal moment that turned Peter Norris Dupas bad. He was an unremarkable child who turned into a lonely teenager self-conscious about his ballooning weight.

Dupas's brother and sister were much older and his mother and father, who were old enough to be his grandparents, treated him as an only child.

He was shy to the point of timidity. No-one imagined he harboured violent sexual fantasies until, aged fifteen and still at school, he attacked his female neighbour in October 1968.

The neighbour, who had returned from hospital just a few weeks earlier with her new baby, answered a knock at her back door. It was Dupas, still in his Waverley High School uniform.

He asked if he could borrow a small knife to peel some vegetables. 'I remarked to him about him peeling the potatoes for his mother and what a good boy he was.'

Dupas then attacked, slashing her fingers, neck and face. He was put on probation for eighteen months and given psychiatric treatment. It didn't work. Nothing ever would.

For more than 30 years he continued to commit sex crimes – and he became progressively more violent. Therapy didn't help and jail delayed rather than stopped the pattern. Each time he was released it would begin again – often within days.

For a few years after his first attack Dupas maintained a pattern of low-level sex-related offences. He was found hiding in the backyard of an Oakleigh house watching a woman undress in March 1972. Two years later, he was caught in the female toilet block at the McCrae Caravan Park watching women shower.

But he had already turned from pest to predator and in 1973 he began to attack strangers in their homes. He would knock on the door, pretend to have car trouble and then ask the woman if he could borrow a screwdriver. In one case, he threatened to harm a woman's baby if she attempted to fight.

114

One detective who investigated the crimes felt that Dupas was only completing his apprenticeship in violence.

Senior Detective Ian Armstrong first interviewed Dupas in the Nunawading police station on November 30, 1973.

For all his aggression to women, Dupas was weak and compliant when confronted, and the experienced Armstrong thought a few stern words would make the quivering suspect confess readily. But Dupas had built watertight doors in his brain where he could lock away his secrets.

'We tried everything and he would get to the point where he was about to talk. Then something would snap and he would go blank, then deny everything,' recalled Armstrong.

Homicide squad detectives 26 years later saw the same pattern during questioning. Shaking, sweating and then just a blank look as the door closed, quarantining his dark soul from the light of his inquisitors' questions. After that there would be the pointless denials or deathly silence.

Once, he appeared at the point of tears and then his eyes went dead – as did the line of questioning. It may have been a way of avoiding police questions or, more likely, his way of refusing to admit to himself what he had done and what he had become.

Would you look in the mirror if you knew a monster would stare back?

According to Armstrong, 'He stood out. To me the guy was just pure evil. He committed a rape in Mitcham and would have committed more given the opportunity. He looked so innocuous but he was a cold, calculating liar.

'His attacks were all carefully planned and he showed no remorse. We could see where he was going. I remember thinking, "This guy could go all the way" (to murder).'

So convinced was the experienced detective, that he wrote on Dupas's file: 'He is an unmitigated liar … he is a very danger-ous young person who will continue to offend where females are concerned and will possibly cause the death of one of his victims if he is not straightened out.'

Police can be harsh judges, but legendary prison psychiatrist Dr Allen Bartholomew, was just as alarmed. He noted that Dupas refused to admit his problems. 'I am reasonably certain that this youth has a serious psycho-sexual problem, that he is using the technique of denial as a coping device and that he is to be seen as potentially dangerous. The denial technique makes for huge difficulty in treatment.'

Despite Bartholomew's warnings that Dupas was 'a danger to female society', he was released from prison in September 1979. Two months later, he attacked four women in just ten days.

This time Bartholomew had no hesitation in declaring that Dupas was a potential killer.

Bartholomew could not resist an 'I-told-you-so' report, pointing out that his view had been ignored. 'The present offences are exactly what might have been predicted,' he wrote when Dupas was again charged with rape and assault.

He concluded that Dupas was unlikely to change. The trained psychiatrist and the experienced detective, Ian Armstrong, both saw something in this harmless-looking man that compelled them to commit to paper their fears that he was a potential killer. Bartholomew warned that Dupas's increasingly violent rapes and knife attacks 'could have fatal consequences'.

Even parole officers who had believed Dupas could change began to give up hope.

'There is little that can be said in Dupas's favour. He remains an extremely disturbed, immature and dangerous man. His release on parole was a mistake,' a parole officer wrote in a report added to Dupas's file in September 1980.

He was released again on February 27, 1985 and within a week raped a 21-year-old woman who was sunbathing at Rye Back Beach. It was not far from where he was found to have spied on women showering at a caravan park more than a decade earlier when he was just learning his trade.

The beach rape was also near the spot where a woman sunbather was murdered in remarkably similar circumstances only weeks before.

Helen McMahon was bashed to death on the Rye Back Beach on February 13, 1985. Her body was found naked, covered only by a towel, and her murder was never solved.

Dupas would have been a prime suspect except he had an airtight alibi that immediately discounted him from the initial investigation. He was not due for prison release until two weeks after the murder. But years later investigators would check the files and find that Dupas was on pre-release leave and living in the Rye area when Helen McMahon was killed.

She was bashed on the right side of her head, above her eye, a trademark injury of Dupas's victims. She was also sunbathing topless and police say female breasts have been a key trigger point for Dupas's violent attacks. Detectives now have little doubt that she was his first known murder victim.

While in jail, Dupas met and married a female nurse, sixteen years his senior. They married in Castlemaine Jail in 1988 while he was still a prisoner.

He told parole officers his marriage to a 'beautiful person' would help him stop sexually offending. It didn't.

He was released in 1992 and his wife, Grace McConnell, was already asking herself why she had married – a question that must have struck everyone who knew her. While still in jail, Dupas engineered a transfer to a new prison, forcing his new wife to move away from her established social circle. He wanted her to treat him as the centre of her universe.

It was a sign of things to come. When he was released, she found him self-obsessed, a snob, lazy and needy. She said if she spoke to anyone for more than twenty minutes on any subject of interest to her, he would interrupt and ask why they were not talking about him. 'Dupas was a possessive, quietly domineering man. He was immaturely jealous of all my friends and anything I did that did not include him as the focus.

'A conversation with him was like talking to a parrot,' she said. Parrots would be justified in being offended at the comparison.

'Our sex life was very basic, almost non-existent. I would go along with it out of a sense of responsibility … It got to the stage where I could not bear him touching me,' she told police.

She was working as an assistant at a special accommodation residence in Woodend and Dupas started 'whining about how much I had to do at the lodge'.

On New Year's Eve 1993, Dupas's wife agreed to sleep overnight at work to look after the residents. But Dupas wanted her to go to a local party with him. Like a spoilt child, he followed her around the home complaining that she should be with him rather than caring for the sick.

Finally she could take no more and told him to 'piss off, get out of my sight, go to the party, go do anything, just don't come near me'. He quickly apologised but the damage was done. The marriage was over and he began to sulk. Rejection triggered his evil alter-ego and within 48 hours he burst into a women's toilet at Lake Eppalock near Bendigo and attempted to abduct a woman at knifepoint.

This was no impulse attack. Like most of his offences it was coldly planned. He was wearing a balaclava when he followed the victim into the toilet block, where he threatened her and cut her with a knife. Police later found handcuffs, knives and a shovel in the boot of his car.

She almost certainly would have been murdered if her boyfriend, a federal policeman, hadn't been close enough to hear her screams.

After a short car chase the boyfriend calmly held him until local police arrived. When he spotted the uniformed police, Dupas yelled, 'They're hurting me,' as if he were the victim.

EVERYONE knew that Dupas was a hopeless case – a man who would continue to offend until he was dead or too old to attack. The State Government had introduced a law that enabled courts to sentence serious repeat sex offenders to indefinite jail terms. It could have been called the Dupas Law as it seemed to fit him so perfectly.

But Dupas's lawyers and the prosecution cut a deal where the sex offender would plead to downgraded charges and the victim would be able to avoid the trauma of giving evidence. He agreed to plead guilty to false imprisonment and in return the prosecution dropped the more serious charges of kidnap, assault with a weapon and indecent assault.

The reduced charges placed him just under the level where he could be sentenced to an indefinite term.

The decision, however seemingly logical at the time, made it inevitable he would be freed to offend again.

But two months before the Lake Eppalock assault there was a murder in the area that police say has all the hallmarks of a Dupas attack.

Renita Brunton, 31, had been married a second time for just six months when she was stabbed to death on November 5, 1993.

She was a part-time religious instruction teacher and the mother of a three-year-old boy. She had owned the recycled clothes shop, Exclusive Pre-Loved Clothing, in Link Arcade, Sunbury, for a year but had recently put the business on the market.

Customers found the shop locked at 2pm with a sign on the door: 'Back in five minutes'.

A neighbouring shopkeeper entered the store through the unlocked back door and found the body about 5pm. Renita Brunton had died of multiple stab wounds to the upper chest and neck.

One suspect seen in the area was described as 173–175cm tall, of chubby build with a fat stomach, short grey-brown hair, bald on top, oval-shaped face and wearing glasses.

In May 1993 Renita had married her husband, Robert, and they lived in Woodend where the couple became members of the local Anglican Church.

They bought a home in East Street and Dupas lived in a rented brick veneer house in South Road, just over a kilometre away.

But Sunbury is more than twenty kilometres from Woodend. How would Dupas know where the woman worked?

Dupas's wife tried to keep order in her house despite the needy nature of her spoilt husband. Once a month, the day after pension day, she would do the household shopping and her husband would always go for the drive – to Sunbury.

The coroner was told Renita Brunton had been last seen in the Sunbury shopping centre between 1pm and 1.15. It was her habit to close the shop around this time to do a few chores, including doing the banking for her small business.

She was found fully clothed and had been stabbed 106 times. She also suffered a fractured skull from a severe blow. The head wound was similar – but not identical – to those suffered by many women attacked by Dupas. The frenzied stabbing was also typical of his methods.

The murder remains officially unsolved although Dupas is the main suspect.

Nobody knows how many women he stalked over the years but experts believe there would be hundreds. Most times he would pull out if he thought he could be caught or if he felt there were males in the area. But if he felt he was in control, he would attack – and kill.

He was released over the Lake Eppalock assault on September 29, 1996, just over a year before the murder of Mersina Halvagis.

On release, he moved into a rented home in Pascoe Vale and eventually established a de facto relationship with a confident South African woman who was unaware of her new boyfriend's hidden side.

She felt the relationship was normal, but privately he brooded that she dominated him. Too self-centred to see her point of view and too weak to confront her, he grew increasingly bitter. When she returned to South Africa for four months from September 21, 1997, until January the next year, Dupas was alone.

And the cycle began again. Rejection, self-pity, brooding and then murder.

'TAYLOR' was a single mother in her late 30s, with a son and a daughter, who wanted to raise a deposit to buy her own home.

So after 'chickening out' a few times, she finally built up the courage to contact a phone sex line to offer her services.

At first it seemed like easy money and over months she trained herself to be non-judgmental when she received phone calls from the lonely to the loopy.

Most of those calls didn't worry her, but now – years later – there is one caller she cannot forget.

He was desperate to talk to an older woman so Taylor bumped her age up fourteen years and instantly became a broad-minded 55-year-old for the caller who had pre-paid her agency for a 30-minute chat.

She still wishes she had not been so obliging and had just hung up.

He started, 'Do you know what I did to the bitch?'

He muttered of pressing down on the neck of a woman and cutting around a breast. 'He liked blood. You could tell that he liked it. When he spoke of the blood, he breathed differently and sounded excited.'

Taylor told police four years later that as his ramblings became more graphic, her mood changed from revulsion to fear: 'I was petrified'. She hung up but the man immediately rang back and said, 'Don't hang up. I know where you live'.

She said he became increasingly excited as he described in vivid detail stabbing a woman. Taylor didn't believe the man was living out a twisted fantasy. '(He) made her seem like a real person.

'He never said the word "knife". He either used the word "steel" or "blade".

'I called him a "sick prick" and hung up. I picked the receiver up and he was still there ... I pulled the plug out of the wall and went to see my children.'

Police say the detailed description of stabbing and mutilating a woman almost perfectly described the wounds inflicted on a prostitute whose body had been dumped on the outskirts of Melbourne.

Margaret Maher was a streetwalker whose mutilated body was discovered in Somerton on October 3, 1997. The wounds were grouped in the breast area in what was a trademark Dupas attack.

He was later convicted of her murder and sentenced to life with no minimum.

Coincidence?

Police checks of telephone lines have identified two calls between Taylor and Dupas. Both were made on November 1, 1997, the day of Mersina's murder – one at 12.45am and the second at 5.14pm, less than an hour after the killing.

IT WAS the tragic case of Nicole Patterson that proved – too late – that the experts were right and it had been inevitable that Dupas would progress to murder.

Nicole was a popular psychotherapist who tried to help young people battle drug addiction.

In early 1999, Ms Patterson, then 28, decided to broaden her client base and converted the front bedroom of her house in Harper Street, Westgarth, into a consulting room.

She advertised in local newspapers and on March 3 a man calling himself 'Malcolm' telephoned. Over the next five weeks he rang her fifteen times before finally making an appointment for 9am on April 19, claiming he needed treatment for depression.

Police believe Dupas knocked on the door at 9am and was ushered into the consulting room.

Nicole made plunger coffee and entered the room with cups, sugar and milk. Then, without warning, he attacked, stabbing her at least 27 times.

She managed to scratch his face and was heard yelling before she was overpowered.

After the murder, he searched the house for any evidence that he had been there. He missed her diary, which was under clothing on the couch in the living room. It had details of the 9am appointment and a phone number.

It would lead police to Dupas.

When police raided his home three days later, they found the newspaper advertisement for Nicole's psychotherapy sessions with her name handwritten by Dupas on the border.

They also found a blood-splattered jacket. DNA tests established the blood was 6.53 billion times more likely to have come from Nicole Patterson 'than from an individual female chosen at random from the Victorian Caucasian population'.

They discovered a black balaclava and a front page of the

*Herald Sun* report on the murder. The picture of Nicole had been slashed with a knife.

The head of the investigation, Detective Senior Sergeant Jeff Maher, (no relation to previous victim Margaret Maher) said of Dupas, 'He was pure evil. He was not physically intimidating but he really sent shivers up your spine'.

Maher said Dupas refused to talk of the crime or co-operate with the investigation in any way. 'Nothing he did was on impulse. Everything was planned in the most calculating manner.'

FBI expert John Douglas says each serial killer has a 'signature' that links his murder victims. Nicole Patterson and Margaret Maher were killed in almost identical ways.

In another bizarre coincidence, the Patterson and Halvagis families had long been associated. Nicole's father Bill and George Halvagis are old mates. They watched their children grow up together when they lived in Warracknabeal in country Victoria in the 1970s, but they lost touch over the years. Now they are linked by a shared grief and one killer.

There is yet another murder where Dupas remains the only viable suspect, that of 95-year-old Kathleen Downes, stabbed to death in a Brunswick nursing home on December 31, 1997.

Phone records show someone rang the nursing home from Dupas's house in the weeks leading up to the murder. Police say the elderly woman was the victim of Dupas's simmering rage over his older wife's rejection exactly four years earlier, when she'd been working at a nursing home.

Dupas also had a prior conviction for attacking an elderly woman. On November 18, 1979, he dragged an elderly woman into a vacant block and stabbed her.

NO-ONE can doubt that Dupas is a serial killer but the question that police want put to a jury is: did he kill Mersina Halvagis?

With no eyewitness and no compelling DNA the police case is largely built on similar-fact evidence that the wounds to Halvagis, Patterson and Maher were so similar that they must have been committed by the same offender.

It was this type of evidence that helped convict him of the Margaret Maher murder after a Supreme Court jury was told the wounds to her were virtually identical to the injuries found on Nicole Patterson.

Pathologist Professor David Ranson has found a series of similarities in the fatal wounds inflicted on Margaret Maher, Nicole Patterson and Mersina Halvagis. In each case, the attack was concentrated on the breast area and each victim suffered a severe blow near the right eye.

Some police believe Dupas was reliving his first murder – Helen McMahon on the Rye Back Beach in February 1985.

But there was another case where similar wounds were inflicted. In October 1969, someone broke into the mortuary of the Austin Hospital and mutilated the bodies of two elderly women using a razor-sharp pathologist's knife.

There was also a strange slash wound to one thigh. The same wound was found on Nicole Patterson 30 years later. Mersina also suffered similar wounds to her right thigh and a slash near the left knee.

Weeks before the Nicole Patterson murder in April 1999, Dupas finally decided to buy his own home and placed a deposit on a house a few streets from the Austin Hospital and a short walk from where the bodies were mutilated.

An analysis of the damage to the clothing worn by Mersina Halvagis and Nicole Patterson shows the knives used in the attacks were similar although it is impossible to say if they were identical.

Forensic scientist Jane Taupin concluded: 'There were multiple stab-type cuts detected in the clothing of Mersina

Halvagis. These cuts were similar in profile to the multiple stab-type cuts detected in the clothing of Nicole Patterson.'

Professor Donald Thomson is a psychologist and barrister considered an expert in profiling. He found clear patterns in Dupas's behaviour and in the way he stalked and attacked women.

He said a feature of his attacks was that 'Most were calculated and planned, they were not opportunistic offences. Dupas staked out either a place or a victim.' Thomson found that he did not continue his carefully-planned sex attacks if he thought there was a risk of being confronted by another man.

He said the crimes were invariably 'located in proximity to places where Dupas had lived, went to school or had worked.'

He said Dupas always used the same method, used a knife, and selected his victims when they were at their most vulnerable.

'An analysis of the deaths of Helen McMahon, Renita Brunton, Margaret Maher and Mersina Halvagis suggests that these deaths are consistent with the features identified in the offences for which Dupas was convicted.'

Police had long known that Dupas would establish a beat where he would wait for the opportunity to attack, as he had at Rye years earlier.

But they needed to find if he visited the cemetery for any reason before the murder.

When he was interviewed, he told police he had never been to the cemetery as he had no relatives or friends buried there. But he lied.

Once, when driving past the memorial park with one of his few friends Dupas had said, 'My grandfather's buried in the cemetery somewhere'.

Police found that his grandfather was buried there about 100 metres from the Halvagis grave.

He lived about a kilometre away in Pascoe Vale, drank at the

First and Last Hotel, across the road from the cemetery and almost certainly drove past the memorial park each weekday on his way to work in Thomastown.

Detectives have established that the wounds inflicted on Mersina Halvagis were similar to those found on other Dupas victims, that he lived in the area and had a reason to visit the cemetery.

But to fit the 30-year pattern of Dupas's sex crimes, police would have to find that he haunted the area planning his attack.

IT took Stefanie Pawluk more than seven years to finally build up the courage to phone the police and tell them the reason she no longer went to Fawkner Cemetery alone.

She was at her mother's grave in the Ukraine section when she saw a man walking fast and looking around as if to see if anyone was watching. She thought, 'This is very strange, he is coming straight towards me.'

She was so concerned that she left the grave, hopped in her car and locked the door. 'I looked up and saw that he had followed me to the driver's door of my car. He stood very close to my car and just looked at me. I was very frightened.'

The man had blond hair and wore glasses. Years later, she saw Dupas's picture on the television news. 'I said out loud, "Oh my God, I think that's him".'

Janet Morton is not the sort of woman who scares easily. She says she has only been truly frightened twice in her life. The first time was when she was nearly hit by a train. The second was when a man in the Fawkner Cemetery stalked her.

Around August 1997, her husband dropped her at the cemetery where she was researching her family tree.

She saw a podgy man staring at her and she smiled, but felt foolish when he ignored her greeting. She moved to another section of the cemetery and saw him again. When she moved a further 50 metres, he followed her. Mrs Morton moved to another section of the memorial and had her head down reading the graves when she heard a noise and looked to her left. 'I saw the same man coming straight at me with a look in his eyes that really frightened me.'

She put up her left hand, started to walk backwards and might have yelled or screamed. Mrs Morton said he stopped and had a 'rabbit in the spotlight look' then moved and hid in some nearby bushes.

'I could see his feet below the two bushes that he was standing behind. I turned and ran as fast as I could and I recall I even jumped over one of the gravestones.'

She ran down the middle of the road inside the cemetery only slowing when she ran out of puff and saw people in the distance.

'This man frightened me so much that it took me about six years to return to that spot to complete my research.'

Years after the incident she was flicking through the paper when she saw a photo of Dupas. Her response was instantaneous. She turned to her husband Ross and said, 'That's the bastard that day in Fawkner'.

On October 5, 1997, Seval Latif was sitting at her father's grave and crying when she felt 'a horrible sense of danger'.

She looked up and saw an overweight man four metres from her on the left 'striding along the road purposely and I felt he was trying to get me with my head down'.

She stood up and he appeared intimidated and moved a short distance away. She headed back to her car but the man followed and stopped to stare through the car window.

In August 2000, she contacted the homicide squad after she saw Dupas's picture in a newspaper. 'I knew he was the man in the cemetery.'

A week before Mersina Halvagis was murdered, Enza

Romanella was visiting her husband's grave when she was approached by a man who wanted help to find the spot where a relative's ashes were kept.

At first she tried to help but something about the man made her scared and she cut the conversation short. In 2000 she saw Dupas's picture on television. She says it was the man who approached her at Fawkner.

Patricia Nemeth was another mourner who saw a stranger heading towards her at the cemetery. 'I immediately felt he was going to hurt me.' It was not his mousy brown hair or his gold-framed glasses that made him stand out. 'It was his eyes, they were blank. There was something peculiar about him. He was evil-looking.'

She stopped going to the cemetery – 'I am terrified to go back' – and when much later she saw Dupas's picture in the paper she told her family, 'I know this man. I've seen him, he's the one from the cemetery'.

She was so sickened she could not bring herself to read the article.

HOURS before the Halvagis murder, Laima Burman was working as a volunteer at the Latvian section of the cemetery when she was approached by a man who said he had just found his adoptive mother's grave.

She later helped produce a computer image of the man. It has a striking resemblance to Dupas. Later she was shown a photo board and asked to identify the suspect who spoke to her on November 1. She picked three – shots numbers six, seven and twelve – as being similar. Number seven was Dupas.

In August 2000, when on holiday in Echuca, she picked up a paper and saw his picture staring back. 'I immediately kept saying to myself, "That's him, that's him".'

Katica Melink may have seen Dupas just minutes before he

attacked Mersina Halvagis. She was with two other women when she noticed a man wearing glasses within metres of the Halvagis grave on November 1 just before 4pm.

When she looked at him, she noticed he immediately turned his head away.

Years later she saw Dupas's picture on the news and felt he looked familiar. About an hour later it dawned on her. 'He was the man I saw at Fawkner Cemetery.'

She remained silent until the Halvagis family made a last appeal for help in late 2004. 'Now I just want to get this off my chest and tell the police what I saw.'

One glance and a sixth sense of danger may have saved Angela Baran's life when she visited her uncle and aunty's grave on All Saints Day.

She was sitting on the grave in Row M around 3.50pm when she felt someone watching her. It was a man with dyed blond hair, glasses and blotchy skin. He was walking slowly and did not appear to be looking at the graves. It was only twenty metres and a few minutes from where Mersina would be murdered.

Mrs Baran looked away and seconds later glanced back to see he was gone.

Instantly she decided to leave. Police say the decision probably saved her life as he was probably hiding, waiting to strike.

'I felt something was not right. He just vanished. I didn't hear him walking on the gravel and there was nowhere near enough time for him to have walked down the end of the path.'

As she left she noticed a red Telstar in the car park. Mersina Halvagis had just arrived.

Sometime later she saw a colour picture of Dupas in a newspaper. She told a friend, 'Oh my God, that looks like him, he's got the same skin.'

But she said she was not sure because the man she saw had blond hair while in the picture Dupas's hair was brown.

Even when hypnotised by a police expert to pick up any memories hidden in her subconscious she was adamant his hair was 'peroxide blond'.

She could not have known that less than two weeks before the murder Dupas had a hairdresser's appointment where he had his hair blonded.

DOMENICA D'Alberto was a young hairdresser who ran her own mobile styling business in the northern suburbs. She had a loyal and largely female client base, so when a man rang and asked her to come to his home she was hesitant.

But the man was 'very convincing over the telephone that it would be all right for me to go to his house. I think he told me that he worked long hours, therefore he couldn't go to a hairdresser.'

It was Dupas, who was well-practised at sounding convincing to women on the telephone.

From February 18, 1997, Ms D'Alberto cut and styled his hair, visiting Dupas every six weeks and giving him bleached blond tips on every third visit.

'I used to think that Peter was always a bit odd.' She was going out with a policeman and Dupas kept asking questions about him. 'Peter often told me that I was pretty and this made me feel uncomfortable. Peter seemed to take a great interest in my personal life but he never said anything about his own.'

On October 21, 1997 – eighteen days after Margaret Maher's body was discovered – Ms D'Alberto visited Dupas to bleach his hair.

For ten months Dupas had been happy with the style of his hair, but around the time of the Maher and Halvagis murders, he started to pester his stylist to change his appearance.

'It was around this time that Peter one day asked me to change his hairstyle ... He became quite irate that I couldn't do anything with his hair. I recall thinking that I was feeling uncomfortable with his aggressive attitude and I had to say something to try and calm him down ... Peter was just so determined to change his hairstyle.'

Jack Sgourakis is an experienced spectacle maker who owns his own business in Campbellfield. He's had hundreds of clients. One was Peter Dupas.

On November 7, 1997 Dupas went to an optometrist in Mahoneys Road, Campbellfield, and ordered a new style of plain bifocals to replace his long-distance and reading glasses.

During the visit he was examined by Isabella La Rocca. It was a routine examination except she noticed that he had a fresh cut to his left cheek. When she mentioned the cut, he said it had happened at work.

He also told friends who noticed the new glasses that his old pair were damaged in an accident at work.

Dupas was employed at the Blue Diamond Furniture Company as a factory hand. He was one of six men who applied for the job in August 1997 and after the first choice was found to be unsatisfactory, Dupas was given the chance.

On the outside he was a qualified fitter and turner and in prison he was a natural handyman often called on to fix small problems.

He soon settled in at the factory as the man who cut the timber to size before it was sent to the furniture craftsmen.

Like all sixteen staff members, Dupas was instructed that any injury that occurred at work or any damage to private property was to be immediately reported.

All injuries, even down to a splinter, were recorded in the company's injury book and the firm had a standard practice of compensating workers for property damage.

A partner and production manager at Blue Diamond, Mr John Kazakis said, 'The staff are told to report the smallest injury'.

But despite the scratch to his face there was no note of an injury in the company record or of damaged spectacles.

So what happened to the glasses?

A damaged pair was found next to Mersina's body but they probably belonged to her.

Detectives believe his glasses were damaged in the struggle and he later threw them away, making up the story that they were damaged at work as a cover.

But only Dupas knows and he isn't talking.

POLICE say Dupas probably stalked women in the cemetery for three months, waiting until he found one alone and vulnerable.

It could have been anyone – but it was Mersina Halvagis.

One of Australia's most experienced homicide investigators has a surprisingly sympathetic view of offenders such as Dupas. He does not see them as truly evil, rather he believes they are driven by demons they cannot control.

'Does anyone think they want to be like that? They would do anything to be normal. The real bad ones are hitmen who will kill anyone for a price. They kill for money because it is easier than working for a living. They choose who they are. Dupas never had a choice.'

And his victims never had a chance.

Police had built a solid case against Dupas but were shattered in late 2005 when prosecutors told them they were still short. Without a fresh breakthrough Dupas would never be charged with the murder detectives were convinced he committed in the Fawkner Cemetery.

And that breakthrough would eventually come from the most unlikely source.

# CHAPTER 7

# The long road to justice

'The place was full of psychopaths.
To me it was just a matter of staying alive.'

HE HAD heard so many confessions before. Desperate suspects wanting the hardened lawyer to produce that magic get-out-of-jail card from his well-worn book of tricks.

He was no stranger to prisons. His clients – accused police killers, underworld gunmen, fallen footballers, failed billion-aires and successful drug dealers – would call him after their arrests, at any time of the night or day.

But this was different.

This time the lawyer could not give advice then drive home in his gunmetal grey, two-door Mercedes before uncorking a vintage red to dull the day's memory.

This was different because the lawyer was also an inmate and the confession was from a serial killer who shared the same high-security cellblock.

There would be no immediate escape. He would see the killer again and again – every day for fifteen months. And he would have to hide the truth.

Until now.

The lawyer – or, more accurately, the former lawyer – is Andrew Fraser, who was serving five years for cocaine trafficking. The killer is Peter Dupas, who was serving life for murder.

As a convicted drug dealer, Fraser had resigned himself to never entering a courtroom again. But he did return to the Supreme Court – not as an advocate but as a star prosecution witness whose pivotal evidence led to Dupas's conviction in August 2007 for the murder of Mersina Halvagis a decade earlier.

She was just 25 and tending her grandmother's grave at the Fawkner Cemetery on November 1, 1997, when she was ambushed from behind and stabbed to death in what police described as a frenzied attack.

Detectives compiled a suspect list of more than 100 but eventually had only one left – the man with dead eyes and no conscience who, police say, has killed as many as six times.

Without Fraser, it is unlikely that Dupas would ever have been charged with the Fawkner cemetery killing, let alone convicted. While homicide detectives had built a compelling case against the serial killer, Director of Public Prosecutions Paul Coghlan, QC, was not convinced it was enough to put before a jury.

In November 2005, he opened the murder inquest saying, 'Much of the evidence in this case will revolve around Mr Dupas.' But he added that there was insufficient evidence to sustain a murder charge.

There was no forensic evidence, no eyewitnesses and, most importantly, no confession.

Throughout decades of stalking, attacking and killing women, Dupas rarely spoke of his crimes. Police who have interviewed him say he retreats within himself and then, shaking and sweating, denies the undeniable.

Derek
Ernest
Percy

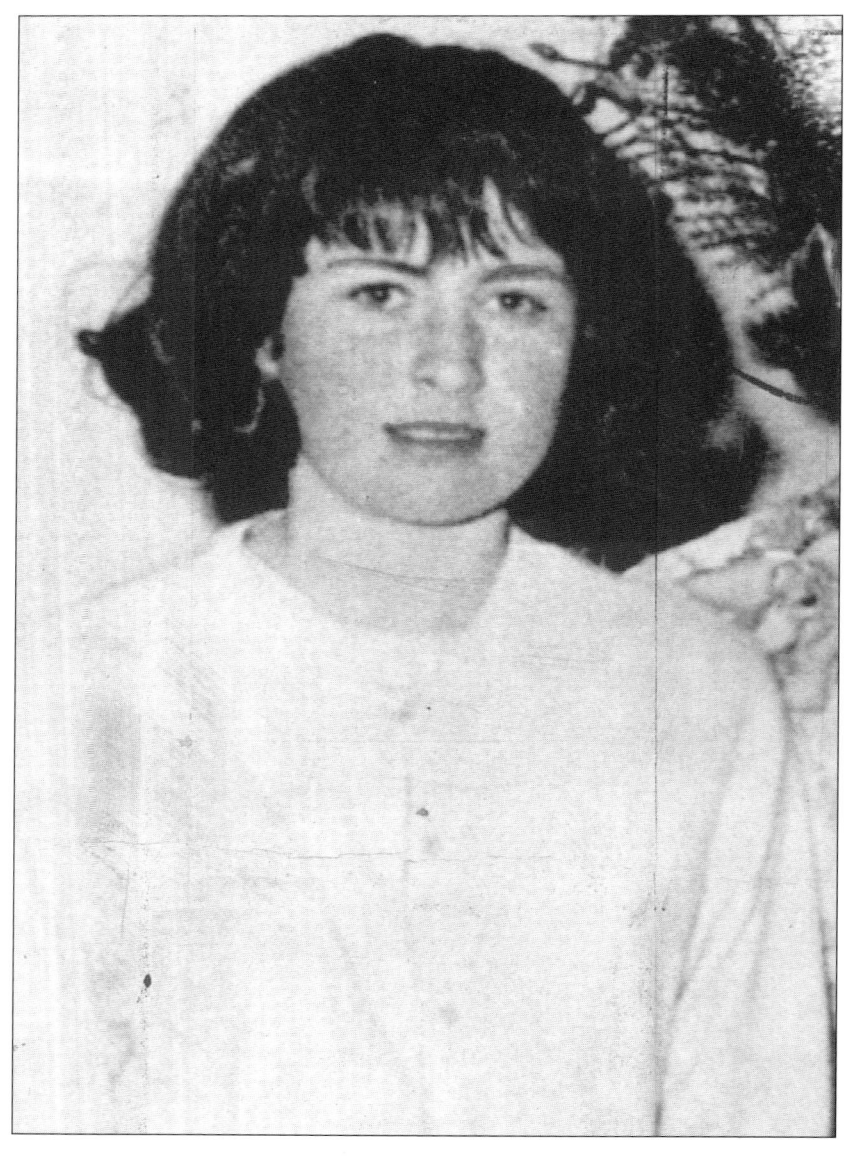

**Marianne Schmidt (above) and Christine Sharrock (right):**
Teenagers murdered at Sydney's Wanda Beach in 1965. Last
seen with youth resembling Derek Percy.

**Above: Derek Ernest Percy (right) at 16 with Mt Beauty High School classmate. A strikingly similar school tie was later used to bind murder victim Alan Redston in Canberra.**

**Left: Alan Redston … was he another victim of child killer Derek Ernest Percy?**

The search: Police and citizens comb the beach for clues after the discovery of the girls' bodies on January 11, 1965. The case was never closed.

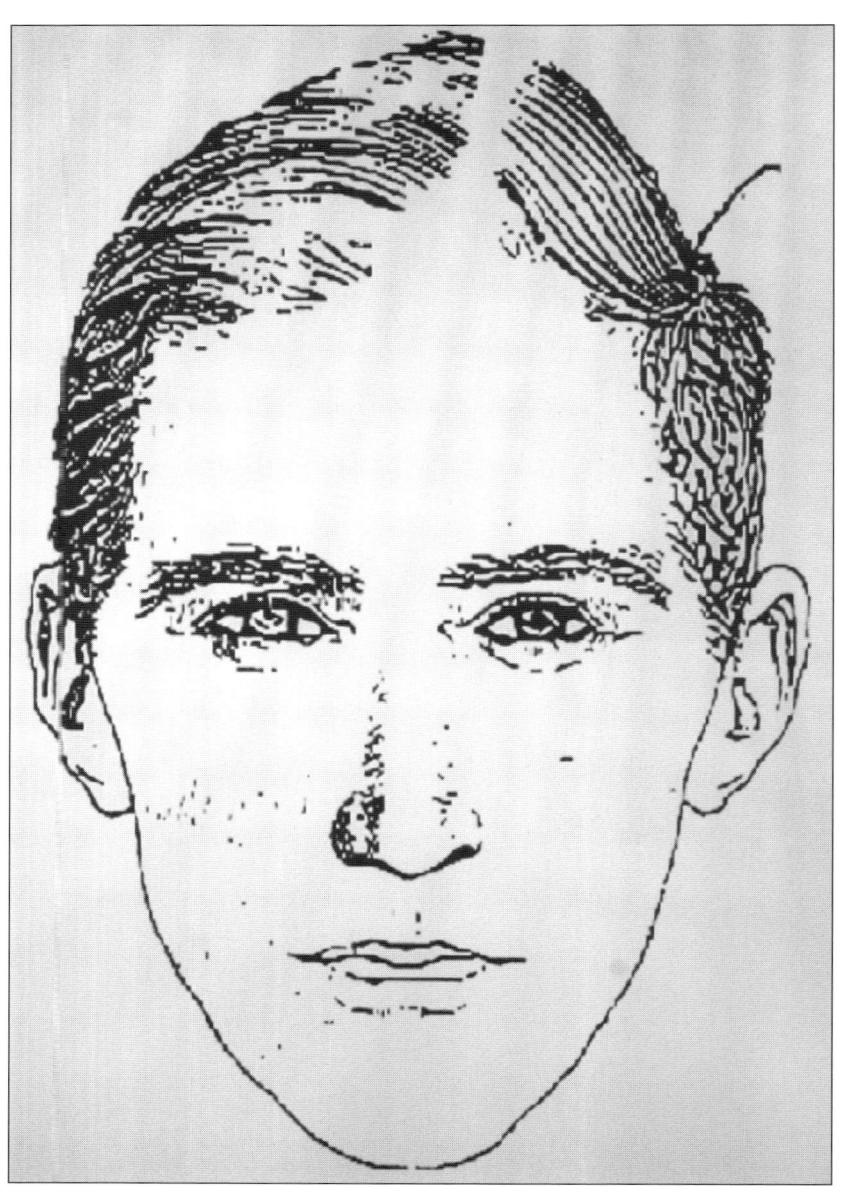

**Identikit compiled from witnesses during Wanda Beach murder investigation.**

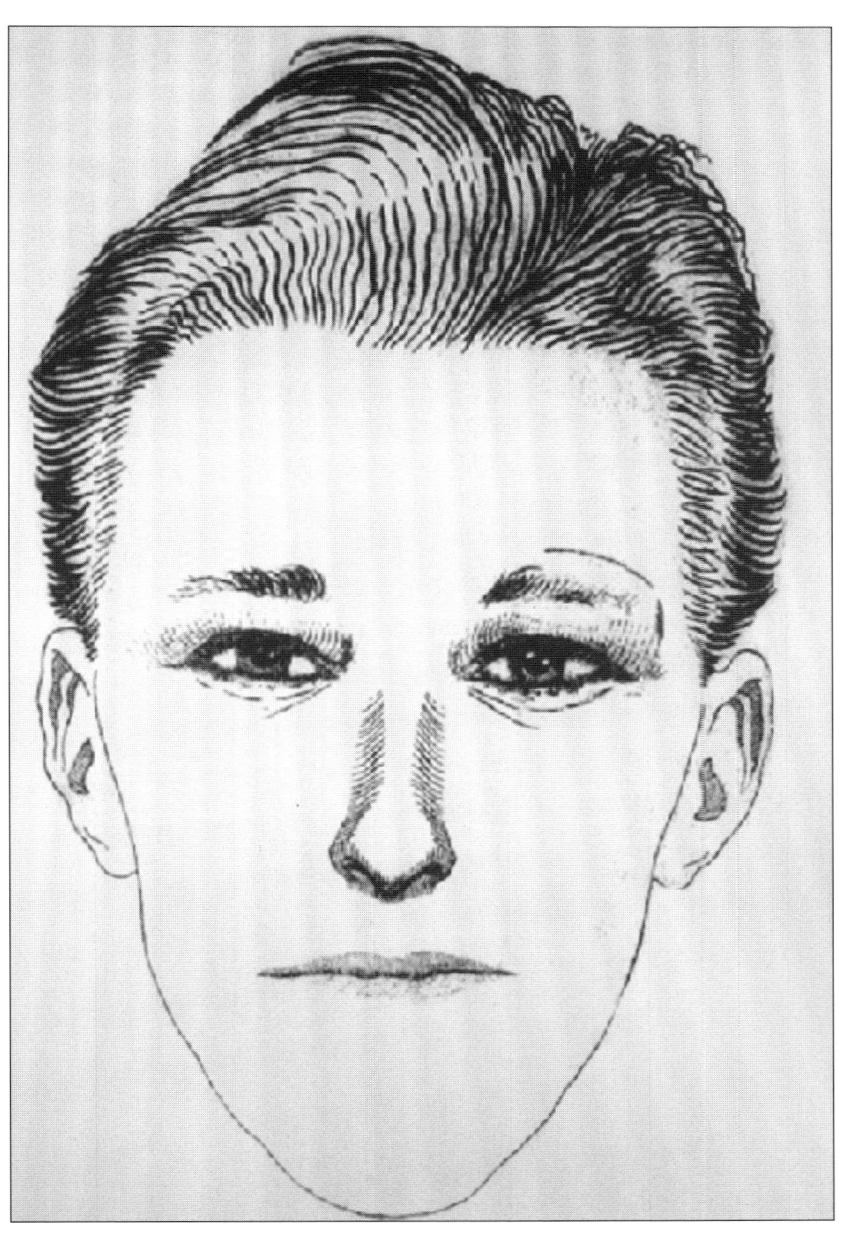

**Identikit of suspect for Alan Redston murder in Canberra.**

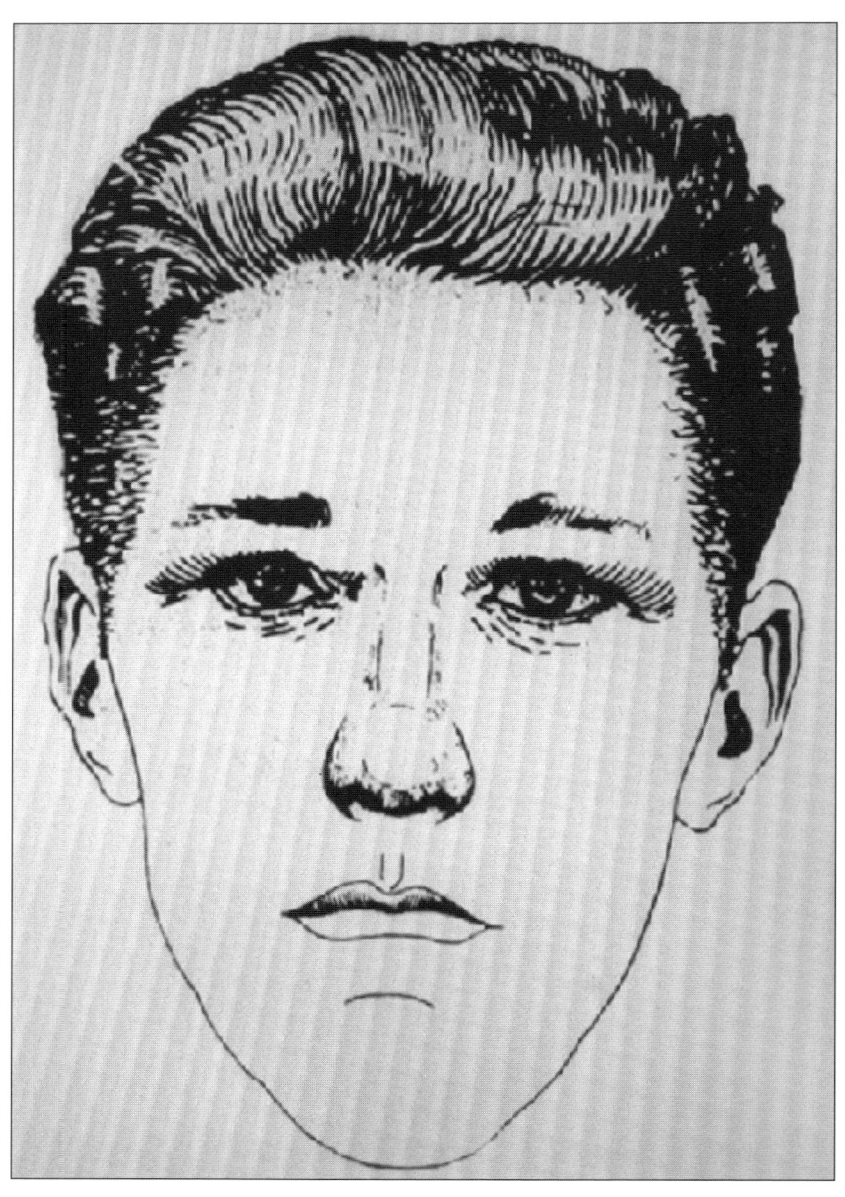

**Identikit compiled during investigation of Simon Brook's murder.**

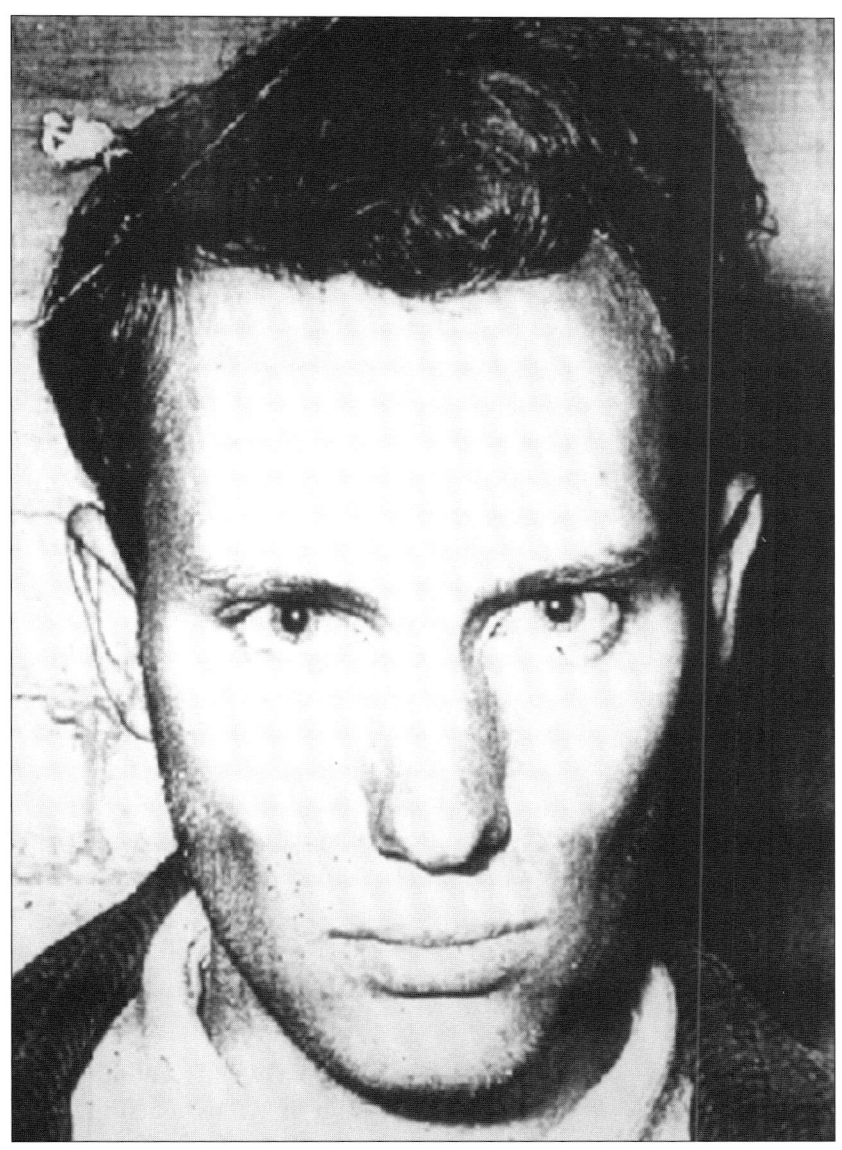

**Derek Ernest Percy after his arrest in 1969: Never convicted on grounds he was insane. This was a blessing as it meant he could be held indefinitely rather than released to kill again.**

Yvonne Tuohy: Taken by Percy from the beach at Warneet in Victoria and murdered. It was the first time police could prove that Percy was a killer, but was it the first time he had killed?

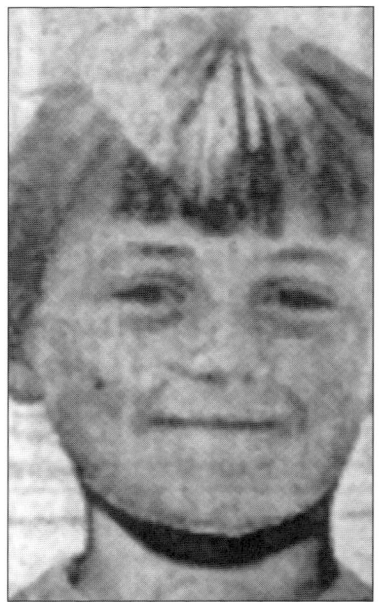

Linda Stilwell: Abducted from St Kilda beach in 1968. Police say Percy is the only remaining suspect.

**Unreliable:** This original artist's impression of the Beaumont suspect was little use because it was based on witness descriptions so vague they hindered the investigation.

**The Beaumont children: When they went missing on Australia Day, 1966, Australia lost its innocence. Derek Percy admits being in Adelaide at the time.**

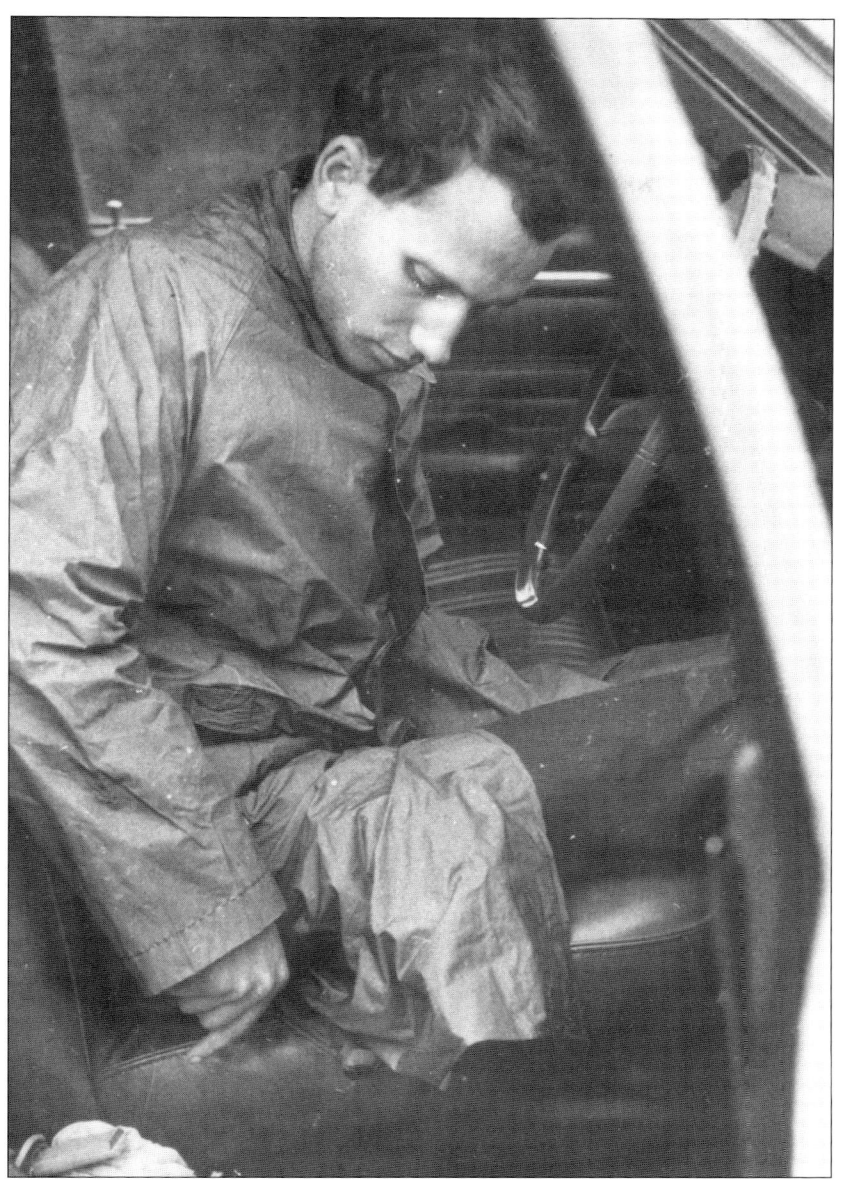

**Re-enactment: Hours after killing Yvonne Tuohy, Percy shows police where he had hidden the murder weapon in his car.**

**Anne Louise Crawford: Murdered, but by whom? The prime suspect walked free.**

**Ron Crawford (right): the luckiest man in Australia walks free with his lawyer.**

Above: A view to kill for ... the angle from which an unidentified sniper shot hardworking transport owner Kevin Pearce at Bendigo. Police know who was behind the hit.

Left: Trouble ahead ... battler Kevin Pearce in collar and tie years before he was gunned down.

But having a top lawyer in his division was too tempting. He began to open up, in halting half sentences, at first seeking advice and later implicating himself – admitting facts that only the killer could know.

When Fraser agreed to give evidence of the jailhouse confessions, it persuaded Coghlan to charge Dupas with the murder. 'Without Fraser's evidence of Dupas's confession there would not have been a prosecution,' he said.

The irony of detectives relying on the word of the former solicitor was lost on no-one, as Fraser was the lawyer police loved to hate. Tough, relentless and a courtroom street fighter, he left many detectives bruised after bare-knuckle cross-examinations. 'I was never a great academic lawyer but I liked a fight and could think on my feet,' he says.

Some were delighted when he crashed and burned because of his $1000-a-day cocaine habit. In December 2001 he was sentenced to a minimum of five years after pleading guilty to being knowingly concerned with the importation of cocaine, trafficking cocaine and possession of ecstasy.

Discredited, disbarred, broke and soon to be separated from his wife, Fraser was a low-risk prisoner – he was a first-time offender, was not violent and was not an escape risk. He could at least expect to spend his sentence in a medium-security country jail.

But someone (he blames old police enemies with long memories) wanted him to do his time hard. Intelligence was fed into the system that his life was at risk and he needed protection.

He was taken in shackles to Sirius East, the maximum-security protection division of Port Phillip Prison that housed up to 38 of the most detested and dangerous inmates in Victoria.

'It was for the worst of the worst and I was stuck there. It was not a place where I belonged.'

He would spend all his waking hours with inmates such as double murderer Raymond 'Mr Stinky' Edmunds, Bega schoolgirl killer Leslie Alfred Camilleri and Dupas – serving life for the murder of Nicole Patterson, whom he stabbed to death in her Northcote home on April 19, 1999.

He soon saw the quality of the company when he met his first roommate – an obsessive paedophile who chain-smoked butts scavenged from bins.

Quickly the lawyer learned the dos and don'ts of life in maximum security. 'You mind your own business, don't ask too many questions and try not to make enemies.'

He would never queue for food 'because you could be stabbed in the neck by the inmate behind you'. If he missed out by being last in line he would slip back to his cell where he kept his survivor's food stash – tinned fish, cheese slices carefully wrapped in hoarded newspaper plastic and dry biscuits.

On his first day in the unit he was about to go back to his cell to avoid alienating one of the division's hard men by sitting in the wrong seat at meal time when he heard a voice call, 'Sit here, Andrew.' It was Peter Dupas.

Dupas and Edmunds ran one clique and Camilleri the other. By sitting with one crew he risked alienating the other and within a day he learned the potential consequences. 'Camilleri chested me on the second day and said, "I should kill you".'

The incident confirmed what Fraser already knew. 'The place was full of psychopaths. To me it was just a matter of staying alive.'

They were to become the jail's odd couple – the ex-lawyer (and schoolboy athlete) and the suspected serial killer. They became the division gardeners and could be seen nearly every day, pottering around the division's small vegetable patch.

At night they would sometimes sit and watch gardening programs on television and read up on horticulture. For Fraser it was a distraction and gave him a chance to get outdoors to breathe fresh air.

A shrewd student of human nature, Fraser soon marked Dupas as a brooder and a schemer: the sort who could take a set against you, then seek revenge with a sneak attack. Fraser thought it was safer to treat him as an ally than an enemy. 'Dupas is probably the most dangerous and unpredictable person I have ever met. He is quite spooky, very quiet and you have no idea what he is thinking.'

While Dupas had a flabby body and his criminal record shows he attacked only defenceless women, Fraser found the killer to be surprisingly powerful. 'He had enormously strong fingers. He could open stuck jars and would twist wire in the garden that others needed pliers to manipulate.'

Fraser had no real interest in Dupas's past.

The former lawyer was determined to live in the present – his plan was simply to survive each day until his release and then try to salvage something from the wreckage of his life.

But as time dragged on, he was slowly sucked into the morass of Dupas's mind – learning against his will about the serial killer's crimes.

It began when they were both in the small, wire-covered exercise yard known as the 'Chook Pen' when a 'Greek-looking' prisoner rushed over and starting yelling abuse at Dupas from outside the fence.

According to Fraser, the inmate called Dupas an animal and blamed him for the Halvagis murder. 'The verbal attack was out of the blue and Dupas was clearly shaken by it. Dupas then said, "How does that c... know I did it?" '

Fraser remains adamant Dupas was clearly admitting guilt rather than just questioning the exchange.

A week later Fraser saw Dupas standing in the vegetable garden staring at a window in Sirius West. 'He was starting to shake, a sure sign he was agitated. I asked him what he was looking at and he told me he now knew which cell the abusive one was in and he was going to try and knock him.'

A few days later Dupas confided he knew the prisoner had a doctor's appointment and 'he was going to jump him then kill him'.

He warned Fraser, 'It would be better if I was elsewhere as he did not want me involved. He took the garden fork and put it where it could not be seen near the pathway'.

Fraser decided to break his promise of minding his own business. He quietly tipped off a prison guard and the medical visit was cancelled.


POLICE had long suspected Dupas was a serial killer. They believe that the weird boy who first attacked a young mother who lived next door when he was just fifteen had gone on to stalk women for the next three decades – and had killed at least six times.

Detectives say he murdered Helen McMahon (February 1985), Renita Brunton (November 1993), Margaret Maher (October 1997), Mersina Halvagis (November 1997), Kathleen Downes (December 1997) and Nicole Patterson (April 1999).

But Dupas had always maintained his innocence and launched an appeal (that failed) against his conviction over the Patterson murder.

'In jail, the etiquette is that you never ask another prisoner what they are in for; to be nosey is to invite violence,' Fraser said. 'I did not ask Dupas any questions as I didn't want to be attacked.'

But one day at the back of the small work station a group of the long-termers were discussing their crimes. Edmunds admitted killing Garry Heywood, eighteen, and Abina Madill, sixteen, in Shepparton in 1966 and said he regretted what he had done but was paying the price. A serial sex offender said he was soon due for release but expected he would re-offend. Then Edmunds said, 'What about you, Pete?'

According to Fraser, 'Dupas hesitated and all was quiet. He then haltingly admitted killing Nicole Patterson'.

It showed that, despite suggestions to the contrary, Dupas did not have a mental condition that enabled him to 'forget' his crimes. He was evil and cunning rather than compulsively disturbed. Fraser, the 30-year legal veteran, saw that Dupas showed no sign of remorse. 'His attitude was what's done is done and not to worry about it.'

But Dupas did worry when he learned the homicide squad was far from finished with him. In September 2002, police interviewed him over the murder of Margaret Maher, 40, who had been found dead near the Hume Highway at Somerton on October 4, 1997.

'When he came back from being questioned he was rattled and came straight to my cell,' Fraser said. Dupas had good reason to seek urgent legal advice.

Detectives had told him they had DNA evidence that incriminated him – there was a glove at the scene that linked him to the crime. (Dupas was charged and later convicted of the murder.)

Dupas left the interview convinced he would be charged with both the Maher and Halvagis murders. Under immense pressure, the quiet and suspicious convict began to break his habit of non-disclosure. He confided to Fraser that there was no forensic evidence at Fawkner and none 'with the old sheila down the road'.

Fawkner was clearly the Mersina Halvagis murder scene and the old lady was Kathleen Downes, 95, who was murdered in her nursing home not far from where Dupas had lived at the time.

After Dupas was charged with the Maher murder he handed Fraser the police brief of evidence to read. In their conversations, Dupas continued to gradually implicate himself in the Fawkner murder.

'Dupas repeated he left no forensics at the scene and no-one, not even the deceased, would have seen him as he attacked her from behind as she was either kneeling at or bending over her grandmother's grave – a frank and surprising admission.'

One day Fraser went to the multiple murderer's cell – remembering to remove his shoes before he entered as every day Dupas would paint the concrete floor of his cell with floor polish. As Fraser began to review the brief, Dupas put his fingers to his lips as a gesture to remain quiet.

He then pointed to the intercom that he believed hid a police bug. 'He sat on his bed, hands folded tightly and tucked between his legs. He trembled and sweated and started to rock back and forth as he did when he was agitated.

'He then got up and took a kneeling position like a victim. He then stood up, became bug-eyed and began flailing wildly with repeated stabbing gestures. When he finished he sat back calmly and started watching the television in his cell. I was just stunned. I put it to the back of my mind. I just wanted to survive.'

At the time, police had deliberately held back the information that Halvagis was kneeling over her grandmother's grave. Only one person could have known – the killer.

Later, while he was weeding the garden patch, Fraser found a homemade knife fashioned from a sharpened metal table-tennis brace. He called over his gardening partner. Dupas took the knife from Fraser and moved it up and down.

'He started to sweat and looked (at) me with a very strange look on his face. I was apprehensive at this time and he uttered one word – "Mersina" – and handed the knife back. I have no doubt he was telling me he killed Mersina with a similar knife.' Fraser dumped the knife in a bin but was so concerned he checked the next day to see that it had been emptied.

In June 2003, Fraser was moved out of the division into the mainstream of Port Phillip and then to Fulham at Sale. Two years later, in June 2005, he was summoned to the guard post at Fulham. At first he thought the meeting would be connected with one of the snippets of petty prison politics that helped pass the days, until an officer leaned over and whispered that a homicide squad detective was on the phone.

'I knew exactly what the call was about before anyone spoke,' Fraser said.

On the line was Senior Detective Paul Scarlett, who had spent more than a year re-investigating the Halvagis case and unearthing several new witnesses identifying a man fitting Dupas's description inside the Fawkner Cemetery in the days and hours before the murder.

He had checked prison records and knew that Fraser had spent more than a year in the same division as Dupas. His prison sources had told him Fraser had acted as the suspect's unpaid jailhouse lawyer. The homicide detective made the call with no real hope of a breakthrough. 'I was furious with him, actually. I couldn't believe he would help someone like that. I expected the call to be short. I thought he'd tell me to get lost and hang up.'

But when Scarlett introduced himself on the phone, Fraser simply asked, 'What took you so long?'

Scarlett asked if he could help in the Halvagis case and Fraser said, 'You'd better come and see me.'

Scarlett drove to Sale that night and was inside the prison the next morning.

He soon confirmed that Dupas had finally made admissions, not to an old prison lag but to a trained legal professional who had dealt with criminals for almost 30 years. It was a breakthrough.

Police hoped they now had an outstanding witness who would not be intimidated by the court process and could provide a unique insight into Dupas.

The question was: why had Dupas broken his lifetime habit of refusing to implicate himself? Perhaps he felt that as a solicitor, Fraser was bound by client–lawyer confidentiality. But Fraser was no longer a lawyer and Dupas was never his client. It was therefore an admissible confession and one that could be put before a jury.

For the police, Fraser was no longer the hated strategist who had derailed many of their investigations. He was the man who could help them finally solve a murder and give the long-suffering Halvagis family a little peace. Fraser was keen to cut a deal and the police were prepared to accommodate him. He wanted out and told Scarlett it was 'a ride there for a ride back'.

But it took more than a year to get federal clearance to move Fraser's release date just two months.

He was freed in September 2006 although he still had to report regularly to the parole board.

JAIL has done nothing to knock the sharp edges off Andrew Fraser. He remains argumentative and his sentences are littered with the slang he learned from underworld clients. He is outspoken, opinionated and outwardly without remorse for throwing away a career, a reputation, a small fortune and a marriage over a decade-long addiction to cocaine.

But scratch the surface and the wound is still raw. He loved his job, loved the spotlight and had wanted to be a lawyer since childhood – following the path of his grandfather and uncle. His client list is gone, many murdered in Melbourne's underworld war. (He admits to having liked Lewis Moran, who was killed in the Brunswick Club in March 2004. 'He was an old-style crook who would wear it when he was guilty. I saw him when he left jail and I said "See you later". He said that, no, I wouldn't. He knew what was going to happen.')

Fraser, 56, refuses to play the victim. He knows he can only blame himself for his fall from top lawyer to convicted criminal. He was at the top of his game in the early 1990s when he was first offered cocaine at a party.

He saw it as a trapping of success rather than a trap and like thousands of others became an occasional ('about once a week') user. But by 1999 he was hooked – with a $1000-a-day habit and only just managing to hang out until the end of the court day before using again. 'I was out of control. I have been stupid. I have damaged my family and myself but no-one else. I didn't attack anyone and I didn't steal from anyone. This has been self-inflicted and I just hope people can use my case to show that drugs can bring anyone down.'

His wide circle of mates has narrowed and the long lunches shortened. 'The silence from some people I thought were friends has been deafening.'

But he has learned to value the loyalty of a few above the backslapping of many.

He is fit and drug-free and his days are filled with early-morning runs, hard labour on a friend's farm, making up for lost time with his children and writing his memoirs, *Court In The Middle*.

The Halvagis case created a dilemma for the long-time defence lawyer. Angry at his treatment in jail and believing his sentence was excessive, he relished the irony of the fact that the very authorities that had destroyed his career now needed him to trap a serial killer.

But there was never any doubt that he would give evidence – even though he knew the defence would try to destroy his credibility as the key witness. The past that he desperately wanted buried would be exhumed – his excesses and drug history would again be news. But the fact was, as experienced prosecutors said, if Fraser's testimony had been negated the case against Dupas would collapse.

Predictably, defence lawyers claimed that Fraser was motivated only by money and that he fabricated the confessions to claim the $1 million reward offered in the Halvagis case. They claimed he was a self-serving liar who saw testifying against Dupas as a way to regain part of what he had lost when jailed over drugs. The jury examined Fraser's credibility, returning during deliberation to ask questions about his testimony.

The jury already knew that Dupas was a killer. Usually, an accused's prior convictions are kept from the jury but because of the suspect's notoriety Justice Phil Cummins decided to confront the issue.

He told the jury at the start of the trial that while they may have heard that Dupas had twice been convicted of murder they could not use that knowledge to pre-judge him. He urged them to remember that they should acquit or convict on the evidence they were about to see and hear.

Fraser says he was unaware of the reward until after police first contacted him. 'I didn't have the faintest idea. I just wanted to do my time and get out. You just put one foot in front of the other and try to get through each week.'

The expert negotiator says that if he was motivated by the reward he would have contacted detectives and tried to cut a deal long before they rang him.

The reward was first offered in February 2005 and Fraser did not make a statement until June – when Senior Detective Paul Scarlett approached him. 'Dupas is the worst sort of human you can imagine. I didn't seek to trap him. I just wanted to do my time and slip out under the radar. But once he talked, I had no option but to stand up and be counted.'

As he speaks his mobile phone sounds. The ring tone is from the classic Warren Zevon song *Lawyers, Guns and Money*, to which the lyrics are:

'I'm a desperate man,
Send lawyers, guns and money,
The shit has hit the fan.'

WHEN the jury returned with their guilty verdict against Peter Dupas the Halvagis family was there to hear it. For them it was the end of a decade-long quest for justice.

'Thank you,' whispered Mersina's father George as he hugged a homicide detective who had spent years investigating the murder.

Outside the court Mersina's brother Nick said, 'For ten years our family has lived our sister's death. That was a very small part of her existence. The rest of our existence we are going to remember her 25-year fantastic life.

'For five weeks, we sat opposite a guy who has now been convicted of three murders of innocent women. I don't know how any person could sit in that room with the lowest form of human existence and not get angry.'

The Halvagis trial illustrated the best and worst of humanity. In Dupas we saw the mutated version of the human condition. A man with no compassion, no morals, no remorse and no courage; a man who hunted women as if they were prey and then hid behind silence when he was exposed.

But in the same court was the victim's family, who refused to give up when there were no answers. They fought for Mersina who could not speak for herself. And there were police and prosecutors who kept going even when they knew that Dupas had already been jailed for life and would never be released.

As Director of Public Prosecutions, Paul Coghlan had a budget to manage. It would have been easy to shelve the Halvagis case as too expensive an exercise when the suspect could never be released from prison in any case. But he knew that justice, not a set of numbers, is the real bottom line in the judicial system.

He said while Dupas could not receive a heavier sentence the prosecution was pursued because 'for the Halvagis family it was important to see that justice was done.'

Coghlan, who on the week of the Dupas guilty verdict was elevated to the Supreme Court, said, 'It is likely he has committed more murders (but) cases are about evidence.' He described Dupas as 'one of the most evil people we've ever dealt with'.

The head of the investigation, Detective Senior Sergeant Jeff Maher, said Peter Norris Dupas was 'pure evil and should never be released'.

Senior detective Paul Scarlett said it 'was a great relief that justice could be done for the victim and her family'.

He described the Halvagis family as a wonderful family that deserved answers about Mersina's death. 'Nothing can bring Mersina back but at least they know that the man who did it will never have the chance to do it to someone else.'

# Life and times of a serial killer

*JULY 6, 1953* – Born in Sydney, youngest of three children. Moves to Melbourne with his family when still a baby.

*OCTOBER 3, 1968* – Arrested for stabbing a woman in Mount Waverley with a knife. Given eighteen months probation and sent to psychiatric hospital for examination.

*MARCH 10, 1972* – Caught peeping at a woman through the window of her Oakleigh home. Fined $50.

*NOVEMBER 5, 1973* – Raped a woman with a knife and threatened her baby in Mitcham.

*NOVEMBER 15, 1973* – Questioned after frightening a twelve-year-old girl by repeatedly staring at her.

*NOVEMBER 30, 1973* – Arrested and charged with rape, housebreaking and stealing, and housebreaking with intent to commit a felony.

*JANUARY 1, 1974* – While still on bail for previous offences, and remanded to a psychiatric hospital, arrested for peeping at young girls showering in toilet blocks at Rosebud Beach. Fined $140 for loitering with intent and offensive behaviour.

*SEPTEMBER 30, 1974* – Jailed for nine years, with a minimum of five, for the November 1973 rape.

*SEPTEMBER 4, 1979* – Released from jail.

*NOVEMBER 9, 1979* – Raped a woman while threatening her with a knife at Frankston (while still on parole).

*NOVEMBER 11, 1979* – Chased a woman in Frankston, threatened her with a knife but fled.

*NOVEMBER 18, 1979* – Stabbed an elderly woman in the chest at Frankston.

*NOVEMBER 19, 1979* – Tried to grab a woman in Frankston but she screamed and he ran.

*JUNE 2, 1980* – Sentenced to six years with a minimum of five for the Frankston offences.

*FEBRUARY 6 to 14, 1985* – Given pre-release leave from jail.

*FEBRUARY 13, 1985* – Helen McMahon murdered while sunbathing on a beach at Rye.

*FEBRUARY 27, 1985* – Released from jail.

*MARCH 3, 1985* – Raped a 21-year-old woman at Blairgowrie Back Beach.

*JUNE 28, 1985* – Sentenced to twelve years with a minimum of ten.

*MARCH, 1992* – Released from jail.

*SEPTEMBER 23, 1993* – Attempted to assault a girl horse-riding at Kyneton. Prosecution not authorised by the Office of Public Prosecutions.

*NOVEMBER 5, 1993* – Renita Brunton murdered, stabbed up to 60 times in her Sunbury shop.

*JANUARY 3, 1994* – Attacked woman with a knife and indecently assaulted her in a Lake Eppalock toilet block.

*NOVEMBER 21, 1994* – Jailed for three years and nine months for false imprisonment. The possibility of an indefinite sentence under dangerous offenders laws not raised by the prosecution.

*SEPTEMBER 29, 1996* – Released from jail.

*OCTOBER 4, 1997* – Margaret Maher's body found dumped near Hume Freeway at Somerton.

*NOVEMBER 1, 1997* – Mersina Halvagis stabbed to death while visiting her grandmother's grave at Fawkner Cemetery.

*DECEMBER 30, 1997* – Kathleen Downes, a 95-year-old widow, found stabbed to death in her room in a Brunswick nursing home.

*APRIL 19, 1999* – Nicole Patterson stabbed to death in her Northcote home.

*APRIL 22, 1999* – Dupas arrested at a Thomastown hotel.

*AUGUST 15, 2000* – A Supreme Court jury finds him guilty of the Nicole Patterson murder. Sentenced to life with no minimum.

*FEBRUARY, 2001* – Task force Mikado set up to investigate Dupas in connection with a series of unsolved murders.

*OCTOBER 2, 2002* – Dupas charged with the murder of Margaret Maher.

*AUGUST 15, 2003* – Magistrate refuses to commit Dupas to trial. DPP Paul Coghlan, QC, presents him directly to the Supreme Court.

*AUGUST 11, 2004* – Convicted of the murder of Margaret Maher. Sentenced a second time to life with no minimum.

*FEBRUARY 1, 2005* – A $1 million reward offered for information on the Halvagis murder.

*SEPTEMBER 11, 2006* – Charged with the murder of Mersina Halvagis.

*AUGUST 9, 2007* – Dupas found guilty of murdering Mersina Halvagis.

*Court In The Middle,* by Andrew Fraser (Hardie Grant).

# CHAPTER 8

# Hitting back

If the puncher would not own up, he would gun
for the target he could clearly identify – the
off-duty policeman driving the bus.

HE didn't see who threw the punch, but he felt it. His left eye
was swelling fast and he felt woozy. It wasn't until he heard an
agitated onlooker yelling into a mobile phone, 'Now he's
covered in blood' that he realised he was bleeding so much,
down his cheek onto his white shirt.

All he knew was that someone inside the mini-bus had
snatched his hat and, worse, his yarmulka (the skull cap
orthodox Jewish men must wear) and that when he'd demanded
its return he'd been hit in the face.

What hurt most, Menachem Vorchheimer said later, was
being attacked and humiliated in front of his children for no
reason except being what and who he is. That made him angry.
Months later, he still was. And a year after that, living in a
different country, nothing has changed for him except the date.
He is still angry and he still wants justice.

It started around 6.20pm on October 14, 2006, a Saturday –
not just the Jewish sabbath but last day of one holy festival and

the beginning of another, Simcha Torah, a time of rejoicing and prayer for orthodox Jews. It was also Caulfield Guineas Day, the beginning of another sort of festival, the Spring Racing Carnival, which has its own rituals: mostly involving betting, drinking and the wearing of brightly coloured garments and much fake tan.

Menachem Vorchheimer had been walking west down Balaclava Road from his home in East St Kilda: a slight, bearded figure in a black hat and coat, wheeling two of his three children – Yudi, six, and Simi, three – in a pusher. His wife, Shoshi, was home with the youngest while he took the other two to the Yshiva synagogue for the children's program after 'the usual long family lunch – three or four hours outside in the courtyard'.

The children had been looking forward to lollies, stories and seeing others their own age at the synagogue. This is how the family spent their holy day together.

Then the mini-bus full of rowdy passengers drove past, heading west. Young men were yelling. The young father heard 'Go the Nazis' and 'F... the Jews'. He says one of them mimed a machine-gun sweep, as if to mow down passers-by, including him and his children in the pram. Some joke.

The only word Vorchheimer could see on the bus was 'Christians' and he wondered briefly if it were some weird ultra-Right religious group, cruising Melbourne's Jewish district to persecute people like himself and his family. When he found out later it was the name of the bus line he smiled about the obvious Christians v. Jews joke. But, on the day, there was nothing amusing about what happened next.

Orthodox Jews do not drive on the sabbath and mostly live walking distance from synagogues, so the street was crowded with men dressed like Vorchheimer in black hats and coats and long beards, standing out like the Amish in Pennsylvania, apart

154

from the absence of horse-drawn carts. Inevitably, this attracts comment and abuse – more in recent years than before, a trend that worries Jewish community leaders.

Often, on Friday nights and Saturdays, louts scream insults as they drive past. Usually, their targets ignore it because the abusers speed away.

This time it was different. The mini-bus was fully loaded and slow – and so were most of its passengers, apparently, because they made the mistake of yelling just as the bus was stopping at a red light.

Vorchheimer left the pusher on the footpath and went to the driver's window, demanding to know who they were and if there was anyone in charge who could prevent the offensive behaviour.

He says the driver was surly and dismissive and refused to identify the group or its leader. 'He just told me it was a charter bus.' Passengers would later claim Vorchheimer kicked the bus in anger. If he did, he could hardly be blamed.

It might have ended with that. But the bus mob couldn't let the exchange rest there: it would be too much like being rebuked and losing face, perhaps. As the bus moved off, a man leaned from a window and snatched Vorchheimer's hat and yarmulka. He was mortified.

'I went back to the footpath to the kids,' he recalls. 'Then a grey car flashed by and pulled in front of the bus to make it stop.' As he hurried along with the pusher, he saw someone running towards the bus. This was a man he would later know only as 'Keith', who had seen the hat being grabbed and was angry about it.

Keith was not Jewish, just a good bloke who didn't like what he was seeing, Vorchheimer said later.

By the time Vorchheimer reached the bus, someone else had joined in, too: the driver of the grey car was demanding the hat, his prized Italian Borsalino that had cost him $US180 on an overseas business trip. Someone threw it from the bus onto the footpath near the pusher – but the yarmulka was still missing.

Again he went to the driver's window 'to plead for my yarmulka'. Again, he says, the driver brushed him off – 'and the rest of them were swearing at me'. He moved to the passenger side, and remonstrated with two young men through a window, demanding the yarmulka's return.

That's when the punch landed. He thinks whoever did it was hidden behind the two people he was arguing with. The only clue was that he thought the assailant was wearing a pink tie. He saw his yarmulka thrown on the ground and grabbed it. He had a broken cufflink and his eye stung.

Two women were comforting his sobbing children. A crowd gathered, circling the bus as the driver tried to reverse from the car blocking its path. Everyone who saw it thought it looked like an attempt to escape before police arrived. It was a logical enough conclusion.

Then Menachem Vorchheimer made his stand. He walked to the front of the bus and sat down in its way. That's when the more sober passengers might have guessed that their mates had picked the wrong man. One who fights back ... and who just happens to run a $60 million-a-year company.

THREE police cars came from St Kilda police station – which, like Sydney's King's Cross and Darlinghurst districts, is a place where young police learn fast from streetwise colleagues. In 'the job', as police call their work, to be stationed at St Kilda once meant being in 'the St Kilda Police Force' – a wry acknowledgment that for a long time the station represented the law in a traditionally lawless area, home of Melbourne's red-light district, cheap boarding houses, tough pubs, strip joints and drug dealers, and all the 'punters' that various forms of vice lure from elsewhere. Added to this sometimes pungent brew was the multicultural mix, but especially the relatively high number of observant Jews who live in the area that some themselves refer to jokingly as 'Jew Town': overwhelmingly diligent, law-abiding citizens, but magnets for the sort of stupid, racist abuse that had bubbled over on this day.

The police soon found out that the mini-bus was chartered by a 'punters club' of players and coaches from Ocean Grove Football Club. They also learned something else: that the driver was an off-duty policeman. But this snippet would stay discreetly hidden until a reporter dug it up some days later.

In fact, the police used much discretion in the discharge of their duties. They did not breathalyse their off-duty colleague, presumably because he seemed sober. Nor did they take statements from his passengers on the grounds that they were probably not sober.

This makes sense, as statements from intoxicated people are useless in court. And, at that stage, it must have seemed unlikely that it would end up in court.

Traffic was banking up behind the besieged mini-bus, so it seemed smart to move it on quickly. No-one was volunteering useful information and it must have seemed easier to send the bus home than to take twenty people into custody to try to identify the culprits.

Senior Constable Jim Tzefer gave Vorchheimer his mobile telephone number and assured him 'justice would be done'. Diplomacy and discretion, all at once.

The footballers had come to Melbourne that morning from their seaside hometown on the Bellarine Peninsula, about twenty minutes past Geelong, for a day of punting and drinking at Caulfield races – a classic example of the end-of-season trip, although it was not actually being run by the football club proper.

The driver, Senior Constable Terry Moore, was not a 'local' and did not belong to either the football club or the punters club. He was an acquaintance of an assistant coach, Craig Fagan, a casual connection that Moore must have cursed later when it struck him how much trouble doing a 'favour' had caused him.

The most senior figure on the bus was the playing coach, Matthew Sproule, recruited the previous season from Melbourne's tough western suburbs competition. Sproule handled betting for the syndicate that afternoon. It hadn't been a wild success – 'We turned $200 into $100', he joked later – but that would be the least of their worries. They might have been better off to punt more and drink less.

The group had been joined late that afternoon by another Ocean Grove player who had got to the races independently and hitched a ride home on the bus. Young, slightly built and likeable, with a few drinks on board he turns into what his family calls the 'class clown'.

A son of former Baptist missionaries, he later admitted yelling insults. It's hard to believe he was the only one. It's also hard to believe, but nonetheless true, that his surname is Christian: meaning that a Christian called Christian travelling on a Christian's mini-bus would end up in strife with non-Christians.

The bus left the car park around 6pm, skirted the racecourse and headed west down Balaclava Road through Caulfield towards St Kilda – normally a logical short-cut for anyone heading for the Westgate Bridge and Geelong.

But it ran through Melbourne's orthodox Jewish heartland – on Saturday evening, when the streets would be full of people walking to worship dressed in clothes not seen in downtown Ocean Grove.

It would have been prudent for the driver to warn his rowdier passengers to shut the windows and behave. As it was, the white mini-bus attracted attention before it went past Vorchheimer and his two children. Aviva D., a professional woman old enough to have five children and cautious enough not to have her surname published, saw the bus cross Orrong Road around 6.15pm.

'One guy was leaning with his chest out the window, and he yelled out a crude sexual reference,' Aviva recalls. 'Something like: "I'll take you from behind".' She finds racist abuse worse than sexual harassment, as her mother is a Holocaust survivor. (Later that same night, she says, someone in a car shouted 'Heil Hitler!' and did a Nazi salute.)

Aviva was walking towards St Kilda. When she got to the Hotham Street intersection, she saw the white mini-bus stopped, surrounded by angry people. She wasn't surprised. Later still, walking home, she saw police cars and an ambulance and heard about the assault – which is why she called talkback radio when the story broke a few days later. She wasn't the only one.

Eli Solowiejczyk, too, had been walking near the same intersection as Aviva and heard racist abuse. He later made a statement to police about it and got in touch with Menachem Vorchheimer.

Michael Granek, a member of the congregation at the Mizrachi synagogue in Balaclava Road, began his usual half-hour volunteer security shift on the synagogue door at 6pm that evening.

About half-way through his shift he and the professional security man with him, a former Russian policeman who guards the synagogue every week, saw 'a white mini-bus full of males hurling abuse'.

At the time Granek shrugged it off. 'Drunks drive past and think it's tough to call out "Effing Jews" ,' he says. 'I don't take it personally. It's ignorance, alcohol, bravado in front of their mates, and it happens maybe three times out of four that I am on duty. But this time I heard shortly afterwards that someone had been bashed.' He later contacted both the police and Menachem Vorchheimer.

The Christian's bus from Ocean Grove was not the only mini-bus causing trouble in the area that evening – a fact that would lead to some confusion about the route it took, and led to understandable speculation that a bus full of racist rednecks was criss-crossing St Kilda looking for Jews to abuse.

Some of them might have been racist rednecks but they weren't roaming St Kilda looking for easy targets to yell at. They were just picking on the ones they saw as the bus took its perfectly logical way from Caulfield racecourse towards the Westgate Bridge towards the Geelong Road and home to Ocean Grove.

A Caulfield man, Nathan, who wants to remain anonymous because of his work, was walking down Glen Eira Road – parallel with Balaclava Road —with his young son around 6.15pm when they saw a mini-bus full of men banging the vehicle's sides. 'They yelled "Fucking Jews" at us,' he recalls. 'I would like to get them in a room and give them an earful.'

When Nathan heard of the assault on Vorchheimer, he assumed the group he had seen was responsible. But another witness, Yoshi Aaron, who works for *Australian Jewish News*, had noted details of a mini-bus in Glen Eira Road when its occupants yelled abuse at him and his wife: it was a Thrifty hire vehicle, registered 1377 NE. Not the Christian's bus.

The fact there were two buses on different routes led some people to assume racist thugs were combing the district. As stated, there was no evidence of this. But what did happen was bad enough and Menachem Vorchheimer is not going to let anyone forget it.

# HITTING BACK

THREE months after the battle of Balaclava Road he sits at his dining room table only a few hundred metres from where the incident happened, re-telling his story so far and mapping the campaign ahead.

He has a husky voice and speaks quietly, but lots: words rush out as new thoughts strike. On the table is a pile of papers and folders, notated for ready reference. A tiny scar is all that's left of the cut eye. Feelings are harder to heal.

As he talks, his baby son climbs over him, gurgling happily. Vorchheimer is a fond father; his life revolves around family, faith and work. Each evening he tries to be home to see the three children before bedtime. Each morning he rises early to pray at dawn before going to work at his firm's Dandenong South warehouse, where his 130 employees range across 'maybe twenty' nationalities. 'I'm the only one with a beard and yarmulka,' he says.

He has to make many overseas trips but dislikes being away on the sabbath, because that is time set aside for family and worship. Late in 2006 he left on a Sunday, as usual, and went to Hong Kong, Britain and Singapore but still managed to get home in time to spend the sabbath with his family. Of the five nights away he spent one in a hotel bed – the rest were on aircraft.

This fierce devotion to family could be a reaction to his own troubled childhood, though he speaks fondly of his father, Ludwig, whose influence lingers sixteen years after his death.

Ludwig Vorchheimer fled Germany to avoid the Nazis in 1938, aged sixteen, was interned in England as an enemy alien during the war, then lived in America before coming to Sydney in the 1960s. He married an Australian, Sarah Coleman, a convert to Judaism twenty years his junior.

Surviving the Holocaust turned Ludwig towards the strict orthodox Lubavitch sect. He raised his four sons the same way;

they grew up straddling two cultures. Menachem, the second son, went to Sydney Boys' High before being sent to Melbourne to a traditional Yshiva school.

The boys' grandfather Norm Coleman played rugby league with St George and was a 'Rat of Tobruk' in the Australian Army in World War 2. The family descends from John Palmer, purser on the First Fleet flagship Sirius, later a commissary and magistrate in colonial Sydney.

The irony amuses Vorchheimer: he's one of a tiny minority of Australians to trace their origins back to the First Fleet, yet is heckled by yobs no doubt because they think he looks 'un-Australian'.

As a boy in Bondi, he followed Balmain Tigers ('Benny Elias, Gary Jack') and loved cricket: 'I was a right arm spinner – like Greg Matthews. My best figures were four for six.'

His parents' marriage ended bitterly. By 1988 the brothers had moved to Melbourne with their ageing father, leaving their mother in Sydney.

When Ludwig was hit by a car that year, he was badly brain-damaged and a bedridden invalid until his death three years later. The tragedy cast the boys adrift.

An early sign of the steel in young Menachem was when, at fifteen, he persuaded the Victorian Guardianship Board that he and his brothers and their invalid father should not be under the guardianship of their estranged mother. It was a tough call for a teenager to make but one his mother came to accept.

The boys were fostered by generous Melbourne Jewish families. Emmanuel Althaus, who took Menachem into his family, jokes about it ('We were young and stupid – my wife was young and I was stupid.') but admits it wasn't easy to 'civilise' the 'feral boy' who had been doing the best he could for a long time. He is, however, pleased with the result of his tough love: a good education, good marriage and good career have turned the foster-son into the sort of success story any parents would be proud of.

Menachem says: 'I had to mature fast and stand up for myself. I wouldn't be where I am today if I hadn't had to do that.' At 28 he became chief executive of a textile firm. Now, at 33, he has boosted the company's growth in a way that suggests he will become a business giant.

Which meant that when he turned his sights on the Ocean Grove Football Club and the police force, as one of his targets concedes ruefully, 'he certainly got everyone's attention'.

A SWIFT, heartfelt apology by those at fault would have settled it. But Menachem Vorchheimer thought that the approach made to him was too little, too late, and too cagey to be convincing.

'It's like someone stepping on your foot,' he says. 'If they apologise, you forget it. But if they try to say they didn't do it, or maybe it was actually your fault, then you can't accept it.'

When his telephone rang on Monday, October 16, almost 48 hours after the incident, it wasn't Ocean Grove calling. It was his local member of parliament, to say she had called a media conference. Vorchheimer had spoken to politicians on both sides of politics earlier that day. Each suggested going to the media to ensure that the police and the football club took him seriously.

The story was splashed on the front of the *Herald Sun* next day and got a big run on talkback radio and television. The news hit Ocean Grove hard – people there would still be talking about it months later. But no-one connected with the mini-bus contacted Vorchheimer that morning. And there was already a hint someone was trying to spin the story against him.

A reporter from the *Geelong Advertiser*, Ocean Grove's nearest regional daily, called and asked what his 'version' of the incident was – as if there were some doubt about the facts. The question was absurd: it implied that a prosperous, peaceful, religious man pushing a pram would deliberately attack a bus full of footballers and contrive to have his hat stolen and his eye cut. For what?

Vorchheimer was livid. Someone was trying to smear him to protect the footballers. His suspicion hardened when he heard people were peddling a story that he had 'tried something similar' with Qantas. (This referred to a minor matter years before, when he had challenged Qantas for failing to provide a kosher meal ordered and paid for in advance.)

The next call was from Andrew Demetriou, head of the Australian Football League, making a gesture on behalf of the national game. Vorchheimer was grateful – but Demetriou's urbane and well-timed diplomacy only underlined the deafening silence from the real wrongdoers, with the effect that the Ocean Grove Football Club now looked completely wrong-footed.

'I said to Andrew "Thanks, but it's not your job to fix this up. If you can find my phone number surely they can",' he recalls. The swift response from the AFL left its country cousins at Ocean Grove looking mean-spirited, apathetic and insular. All of which was unfortunate for the football club's president, a local lawyer called Michael Vines.

Finally, late that night, Vines, telephoned Vorchheimer to offer an apology and assurances that he would try to identify who was behind the 'alleged' offences. Vines was well within his rights to try to protect the interests of his players and his club but what Vorchheimer interpreted as a faintly adversarial tone rankled him more each time they spoke.

Vines soon felt the same way about Vorchheimer. Months later, he commented: 'In this country we have a legal system we follow' – rather as if Vorchheimer were a conniving peasant fresh from some corrupt totalitarian state, not an urbane, highly educated Australian like Vines himself. It was, perhaps, an innocent but unfortunate slip.

Vines underlined the fact that the football club had no official link with the punters' big day at the races. Like a principal whose students are caught shoplifting after school, he was stuck with a mess not of his making, half-blamed for something over which he had no control. He was keen to identify offenders but naturally wary of the club wearing any blame for what they'd done. Vines soon scared the younger players: one ashamed lad confessed to yelling taunts, another to grabbing the hat. The problem was that, initially, no-one would own up to punching Vorchheimer.

Vines argued that if a punch had been thrown, a seasoned courtroom veteran like himself would surely have uncovered it while cross-examining the players.

When he did not produce the puncher, he switched tack – urging Vorchheimer to accept that his eye was accidentally 'scratched' in the tussle. This would have neatly removed the threat of an assault charge, no doubt to the relief of all concerned at the football club.

The lawyer – and police – knew that as things stood then, if an assault charge had been laid it would not have stood up in court. But Vorchheimer wouldn't accept the 'punch-lite' theory. From the first week, he saw that the chances of the affair ending with genuine remorse and a handshake were slipping away. If the puncher would not own up, he would gun for the target he could clearly identify – the off-duty policeman driving the bus.

He spoke to his friend Norman Rosenbaum – a Melbourne lawyer famous for his fourteen-year legal battle in New York over the race-hate killing of his brother Yankel in 1991. Rosenbaum said to get a criminal lawyer. He suggested a seasoned barrister, Remy van de Wiel, QC.

The urbane and wily Van de Wiel lives on the other side of

the city, in Clifton Hill. He is not an especially religious man but he has the civil libertarian's dislike of injustice, and the defence lawyer's sharp and sceptical eye for any sign of police misconduct.

On the silk's advice, Vorchheimer studied Acts, statutes and police regulations and concluded that as a police officer, the driver had failed his sworn duty to uphold the law and could be held to account for it. But when he pressed the point with Deputy Commissioner Kieran Walshe the meeting ended abruptly with Walshe insisting that Moore would not be suspended.

It seemed clear that given the festering issue of police working second jobs outside the force, the Government and police command would have preferred to sidestep a showdown with the pugnacious police union over Senior Constable Moore being punished for his alleged lapses as driver of the mini-bus. The other reason to avoid a brawl, perhaps, was that the Government and the police union were making a secret sweetheart deal – for better pay and new handguns – just as the Vorchheimer story broke, a few weeks before the Victorian state election.

Vorchheimer was bemused by the backroom politics and red tape tangled around the case: St Kilda detectives took over the inquiry from their uniform colleagues, the Ethical Standards Division re-investigated the entire affair to ensure the police 'brotherhood' was not looking after its own, and the Office of Police Integrity looked over everyone's shoulder for the same reason. Even the Premier's office had quietly bought into it.

An hour after the tenacious Vorchheimer ambushed Premier Steve Bracks on the eve of the November election, handing him a police statement outlining the assault, he got a soothing call from one Ari Suss – a former Bracks adviser now with the transport king turned developer, Lindsay Fox, but seconded

# HITTING BACK

back to the Premier's staff for the campaign. Fox can afford to be a generous man when he wants to be.

Vorchheimer was polite but unmoved ('Ari Suss is a good Jewish boy – but a politician') by all the promises that everyone was doing their best to see justice done. He vowed to push until he gets a result. And that is exactly what he has done.

Why? It's not about money or revenge, but manners and respect. And about the effect on his children.

His son revealed violent fantasies – of using a laser to shoot the people on the bus and of suffocating the driver. His daughter said they shouldn't go to the synagogue any more because they might get hurt.

But the thing that hit him hardest was finding out that it was his son who picked up his hat and pushed it back into shape. 'He wanted to help his Dad and that's all he could do,' he says. And for the first time in hours of talking, his voice chokes with emotion.

FOR someone who would once have been happy to settle for a sincere apology, Menachem Vorchheimer soon hardened in his resolve to see justice done because, he said, he felt as if he had not been taken seriously enough in the beginning. He reckoned insult had been added to injury and he wanted satisfaction. Because of his dogged persistence, and media coverage, the police force and the Victorian Government had to be seen to act.

It was politic to get results, and results soon came. The police's internal investigators, the Ethical Standards Department, oversaw the investigation of the assault, with a senior ESD officer with lengthy homicide squad experience going to Ocean Grove to re-interview the football club witnesses.

Meanwhile, the Office of Police Integrity, attached to the

Ombudsman's Office, attempted to ensure that the police force investigated the involvement of one of its own: the bus driver Constable Terry Moore – a far more ticklish political problem for both the force and the State Government because of the touchy industrial relationship with the aggressive police union leadership.

The police were keen to nail the footballers for assault. The inference, perhaps, was that this might satisfy the aggrieved victim. If anyone assumed this, they had misjudged Vorchheimer. He wanted the bus-driving policeman's head as well.

Not surprisingly, determined police investigators came up with a better result than the football club office bearers when it came to finding the main offender. Early in 2007, following publicity about the case, they charged three footballers with various charges.

Simon Christian, 21, son of former Baptist missionaries who had served in Africa, was fined $1000 in April after pleading guilty to using insulting words ('Go Nazis' was one phrase) in a public place.

Despite a request from the prosecutor for a diversion order that the shamefaced youngster tour the Jewish Holocaust museum to acquaint himself with the Nazis' handiwork, the Magistrate left it up to Christian to decide whether he would show his remorse by going to the museum with Vorchheimer.

But Christian was never the main police target. James Dalton, 28, a club captain, was charged with theft of Vorchheimer's hat and yarmulka. And, after some keen detective work, Matthew Cuthbert, 23, was charged on three counts of assault and using insulting language. Meanwhile, the Office of Police Integrity found that Senior Constable Terry Moore could have prevented the attack.

When Dalton appeared in court in June, his lawyer requested

a suppression order to hide his family name and address ... on the grounds that the family was the target of race hate mail. The request was refused.

At the time of writing, Dalton and Cuthbert still have to face committal proceedings in the Melbourne Magistrates' Court. If a magistrate finds there is a case against them, they will face trial.

IN MID-2007 Menachem Vorchheimer took his family to live for a year in New York, where he has relatives and friends and was able to land a job. He thought at the time that it would push the incident into the distance, and allow his children to forget the trauma of seeing him attacked. But he is amazed that in New York and in Europe, people he meets – many of them Jewish – recognise him as the Melbourne orthodox man who was punched and abused. There is no getting away from what happened.

But that is not the only reason that going to New York has not turned out to be a wild success. The truth is, the way he describes it in the first few months, they were all feeling a little homesick. His wife misses family and friends in Melbourne. And Menachem and his older boy want to go to the cricket and footy back home. Aussie rules, after all.

Down the street from the family's house in Caulfield is the synagogue where a volunteer called Michael Granek has done security duty for several years. Each year it has become more common for people to yell abuse from cars. But he has noticed a strange thing in the months since the Vorchheimer case: the abuse has dropped away. Sometimes it pays to fight back.

# CHAPTER 9

# Boys with toys

'He became the most dangerous
gangster in Australia.'

MELBOURNE'S bloodiest underworld war began with both a
bang and a whimper in a tiny park in the outer-western suburb
of Gladstone Park near Melbourne Airport.

Gunman, drug dealer and notorious hothead Jason Moran
made two decisions – one premeditated and the other off the
cuff – that started the war that would wipe out his crime family.

Moran and his half-brother Mark had arranged to meet
amphetamine manufacturer Carl Williams to discuss their
mutual business interests. Williams liked to talk in parks and
public places to avoid police listening devices, and the Morans
were happy to meet in an open space where they believed they
could not be ambushed.

The Williams and Moran families had trafficked drugs for
years and while they were sometimes associates, they were
never friends. They often did deals and begrudgingly co-
operated when it suited, but they were also competitors for a
slice of the incredibly lucrative illegal pill market.

While there were many reasons for their hostility, none was big enough to go to war – business was booming. Demand had increased tenfold as amphetamines became a mainstream leisure activity. All dealers had to do was keep a low profile, source their pills and count the cash.

But the niggles remained and the Morans, always quick to take offence, began to stew. At first it was a simple domestic matter: Carl Williams' wife Roberta had previously been married to Dean Stephens, a friend of the Morans.

The next was competition. Williams was undercutting his rivals, selling his pills for $8 compared with the Morans' $15.

The third was business. Williams had supplied the Morans with a load of pills. But he had not used enough binding material and they were crumbling before they could be sold.

The fourth niggle was greed. The Morans claimed ownership of a pill press and said Williams owed them $400,000. Carl disagreed.

The problems could have been settled but the Morans, notorious for their short tempers and long memories, often relied on unreasonable violence to achieve what they believed were reasonable outcomes.

The meeting at the Barrington Crescent park, no bigger than two suburban blocks and surrounded by brick veneer homes on three sides, provided the Moran brothers with the perfect opportunity to remind Williams where he stood – before they shot him off his feet.

It was October 13, 1999, Carl Williams' birthday. He had just turned 29.

Williams was unlikely to have felt in danger – the mid-week meeting was to be held in the afternoon in the open – hardly the ideal place to pull a double-cross. But soon after they arrived Jason Moran pulled a gun, a .22 Derringer. A woman nearby heard a man cry out, 'No Jason' and then a single shot.

It showed the typical arrogance of the Morans. It was daylight in middle Melbourne. Not a dark alley or an isolated spot in the bush. They simply did not believe they could be stopped.

But this time the gunman showed uncustomary restraint. Mark Moran urged his half-brother to finish the job but Jason replied they needed the big man alive if they were ever to get their money. That decision would destroy the Moran clan, and many who were close to them.

If they had killed Williams he would have been just another dead drug dealer and the case would almost certainly have remained unsolved. Instead, Williams became an underworld serial killer determined to exterminate every real or imagined rival he could find.

Williams, who prided himself on being an old-school crook, refused to co-operate with police after he was ambushed. When detectives interviewed him in hospital, Williams said he had felt a pain in his stomach as he was walking, and only then realised he had been shot.

Much later Williams told the author he did not see his attacker. 'I have no idea who shot me and I've never asked … I don't know who did it. Police told me who they think did it but that's their business.' When the author suggested they had nominated Jason he smiled and said, 'You better ask them.'

Roberta Williams gave more away in a later conversation but denied the shooting was drug related. 'Mark was yelling "shoot him in the head", and Jason then shot him in the stomach,' she said.

If the Morans thought that shooting Williams would frighten him, they were horribly wrong. The wound soon healed but the mental scar remained.

The drug dealer began planning his revenge, setting off a very public underworld war that would leave police, the legal system and politicians struggling to cope.

Williams, with his plump, pleasant face, his shorts and T-shirts, did not look like an influential crime boss who could order a death with a phone call.

As a strategist he would appear more a draughts man than a chess man.

Perhaps that is one of the reasons he flew just under the police radar – until he became the most dangerous gangster in Australia.

Police knew he was part of his family's drug business but they assumed the former supermarket packer was a worker and not the foreman.

Like the Morans, police underestimated Williams and his power base. He was ruthless, cashed-up and had recruited a loyal gang of reckless young drug dealers driven by pill money, wild dreams and illegal chemicals.

His team seemed to move from underworld try-hards to big players in a matter of months. Guns, drugs and rivers of cash can do that.

Williams' reputation and power grew with every hit. He began to refer to himself as 'The Premier' because 'I run this fucking state'. But to detectives, he was still 'The Fatboy'.

Police say Williams was certainly connected to ten underworld murders and would have kept killing if he had not finally been jailed.

He will never face charges over many of the murders he arranged after cutting a deal with police that gives him some chance of release one day. His only remaining hope is that he will die a free old man.

Williams' rise from middle-ranked drug dealer to heavyweight killer should never have happened. His plans for revenge and controlling a major drug syndicate should have collapsed when he was arrested in slapstick circumstances six weeks after the Morans shot him.

For Broadmeadows police it began as a low-level fraud investigation and ended as a $20 million drug bust. The fraud involved a local family accruing credit card debts with no intention of repaying, then changing their names to obtain new cards to repeat the scam.

On the morning of November 25, 1999, police arrived at a housing commission home in Fir Close to serve arrest warrants, but no-one was home.

Later that day Detective Sergeant Andrew Balsillie was passing, and noticed two cars at the house. He recalled his team to issue the warrants and, after bursting in, found a pill press, 30,000 tablets (almost certainly the Moran pills that had been returned to be re-pressed) and almost seven kilograms of speed valued at $20 million.

Williams was found hiding in a bed upstairs (his bed attire suggested he was not having a quick snooze – he was wearing a loud, red Mambo shirt).

His father George was found hiding between a bed and the wall in another room, in which a loaded Glock semi-automatic pistol was later found.

Local police rightly chose to run the investigation but called in the amphetamine experts from the drug squad. They were not to know that the two detectives, Malcolm Rosenes and Stephen Paton, were corrupt and would later be jailed.

While there was no suggestion they interfered with the investigation, the Supreme Court later decided that several drug cases, including Williams', should be delayed until the detectives' prosecutions were completed.

It was while Williams was on bail for those (and other) drug charges that he organised the underworld murders.

If the drug cases had not been delayed, Williams would have been jailed for at least four years, unable to carry out a homicidal vendetta.

# The war begins

WHILE inside jail for almost two months on remand, Williams began to plan his first attack, and recruit the team of men he believed would kill for him.

One of the first to join was Andrew 'Benji' Veniamin, the former kickboxer and gunman who once idolised Carlton identity Mick Gatto, a man who for decades has cast one of the biggest shadows in Melbourne's underworld. Williams saw Gatto, who was affiliated with the Morans but not involved in the squabble over drugs, as a potentially powerful enemy.

Williams thought that if he killed the Moran brothers, established underworld figures, including Gatto, would seek revenge. He decided his best chance of survival was not to jump at shadows but cast a bigger one, so he launched a hostile takeover.

Initially, Williams was outnumbered and in no position to take on the Moran brothers, let alone contemplate plans for gangland domination.

Then in a stroke of perfect timing Williams was finally bailed on his drug charges on January 22, 2000. Three days later Jason Moran was jailed for affray and sentenced to twenty months jail. Mark Moran had lost his closest ally and was now hopelessly exposed.

Five months later, on June 15, Mark Moran was killed outside his Aberfeldie home. More driven than Jason and less erratic, he had managed to keep a lower profile.

Until then.

When his death was reported he was referred to as a local football star rather than underworld identity. But police immediately knew it was a gangland hit.

They also knew Mark Moran was entrenched in crime every bit as much as the rest of his family who considered honest work a personal affront. Moran lived in a house valued at $1.3 million. His occupations had been listed as personal trainer and unemployed pastry chef.

Four months before his murder, on February 17, 2000, police noticed him driving a new luxury car. When they opened the boot of the rented vehicle, they found a hi-tech handgun equipped with a silencer and a laser sight. They also found a large number of amphetamine pills that had been stamped through a pill press to appear as ecstasy tablets.

His days as a battling baker were long gone.

In the hours before his death, Mark Moran had been busy. First he had given drugs to a dealer at the Gladstone Park Shopping Centre, 800 metres from where he and his brother had shot Williams the previous year.

The dealer was short of cash and Moran agreed to give him credit. It was not a difficult decision. Few people were stupid enough to try to rip off the Morans.

Moran drove home, received a phone call and left for a second meeting. On returning he was blasted with a shotgun as he stepped out of his Commodore. Williams was the gunman and his getaway driver would later be implicated in another three murders.

Police later established that Williams had only been waiting ten minutes when Moran returned. It smelled of an ambush.

Moran's natural father, Leslie John Cole, was shot dead in similar circumstances in Sydney – ambushed outside his home eighteen years earlier.

But Mark's stepfather, Lewis Moran, was very much alive and drinking in a north-western suburban hotel when he first heard of the shooting.

Immediately he called for a council of war at his home.

The Moran kitchen cabinet discussed who they believed was responsible, and how they should respond. The Morans, never short of enemies, narrowed the field to three. Williams and his team were by no means the favourite. 'We still didn't know we were in a war,' a Moran insider later said.

For Williams it was the beginning, and for the Morans it was the beginning of the end.

Much later Lewis Moran, said to still hold the first dollar he ever stole, tried to take out a contract on Williams but he would offer only $40,000. There were no takers.

There were seven men at the meeting at Moran's home. Five are now dead.

In the case of Mark's death, police suspected Williams from the start, so much so that his house was raided the next day. But internal police politics terminally damaged the investigation. Members of the drug squad, who had worked on the Morans for years, deliberately concealed information from the homicide squad because they believed their investigation was more important than a murder probe they thought would fail.

Their prediction was self-fulfilling.

At the packed gangland funeral (an event Melbourne would see repeatedly for several years) Jason Moran was allowed day leave from prison to speak at the funeral. Mourners said the brother spoke with real emotion but his death notice worried police. It read: 'This is only the beginning; it will never be the end. REMEMBER, I WILL NEVER FORGET.'

Nor would Carl Williams.

Police and the underworld expected that when Jason Moran was released he would make good his implied promise. Williams. But when he was freed on September 5, 2001, Williams was back inside on remand, having been charged in May with trafficking 8000 ecstasy tablets.

The parole board let Moran go overseas because of fears for his life, while Williams continued to recruit from a small area filled with potential killers – Port Phillip Prison.

# The runner

AS is customary when important business deals are sealed, when the man we will call the Runner decided to accept Carl Williams's offer they decided to celebrate with a quiet drink. What made it unusual was it was inside Swallow Unit of Port Phillip Prison and they were drinking smuggled alcohol in the top-security jail.

According to the Runner, it was there that Williams first asked him to kill Jason Moran. Moran had been spotted in London by one of the Williams team (the 'Lieutenant') and, unwisely, decided to return, even though he must have known his life was still in danger.

Williams was not content with one hit team and continued to recruit inside and out of prison. While he was not a great student of history he knew that in a war there would inevitably be casualties and prisoners. He looked to relatives, close friends and hardened gunmen whose loyalty he thought he could demand, or at least buy.

Williams knew that the Runner, no pin-up boy for prisoner rehabilitation programs, was soon to be released after serving his sentence for armed robbery. He was good with guns, and ruthless.

In March 1990 the Runner had escaped from Northfield Jail in South Australia, where he was serving a long sentence for armed robberies. The following month he was arrested in Melbourne and questioned over four stick-ups. As he was being driven to the city watchhouse the detective next to him fell asleep.

When the unmarked police car slowed in traffic the Runner jumped from it and bolted. He was arrested in Queensland in January 1991.

Police claim the Runner carried out 40 armed robberies in

Victoria, SA and WA over seven years. In 1999 he was again arrested after he tried to rob a Carlton bank.

Why the Runner? His trademark was to run into a bank, pull a gun, demand large denomination notes and then run up to 500 metres to his getaway car. His gun-and-run method meant that to police and criminals he was known as a long-distance runner.

Williams believed this running talent would prove useful in ambushes that would probably have to be carried out on foot.

When Williams popped the question the Runner did not hesitate. 'I said yes to show him my loyalty. I was aware of Carl's hatred of the Moran family. Carl told me about an incident in 1999 where Carl was shot by Jason Moran.'

On July 17, 2002, Williams was bailed, despite having twice been arrested on serious drug charges. But the courts had no choice; Williams' case (and those involving six others) was indefinitely delayed while prosecutions against corrupt drug squad detectives were finalised.

Five months later the Runner was released and within weeks he was going out with Roberta Williams' sister, Michelle. He may not have been blood family but he was the next best thing.

The Runner and Carl Williams met daily, and Williams asked his new right-hand man to find Moran. He said Moran was aware he was being hunted and had gone to ground.

'Carl told me that he still wanted Jason dead and that he wanted me to locate Jason so he could kill him. We did not discuss money at this point but I was to start surveillance on Jason Moran.'

Williams' ambitions and his desire for revenge were growing. No longer did he just want to kill Jason. 'Carl developed a deep-seated hatred of the Moran family ... there is no doubt it was an obsession with him. Carl told me on numerous occasions that he wanted everyone connected with the Moran family dead.'

The Runner began to track Moran. With every report Williams would peel off between $500 and $1000 for the information. His former prison buddy was also paid to deliver drugs and collect money, and set up in a Southgate apartment that Williams sometimes used as a secret bachelor pad.

He may have been prepared to wage war in the underworld but he was still frightened of Roberta.

The Runner would tell police that he was not the only one spying on Moran. Williams also received information from convicted millionaire drug trafficker Tony Mokbel, and soon-to-be-deceased crime middleweight Willie Thompson. But more of them later.

Williams and the Runner regularly swapped cars, from a black Ford, silver Vectra, grey Magna and Roberta Williams' Pajero.

But finding Moran was one thing. Killing him quite another. They began to discuss how they would kill their target – the schemes ranged from the imaginative to the innovative and the simply idiotic.

One was to hide in the boot of Moran's silver BMW, remove the lock and spring out to kill him. A simpler version involved lying beneath shrubs outside the house where Moran was believed to be staying. Williams considered hiding in the rubbish bin next to Moran's car, then popping out to shoot him.

It would have had to be a big bin.

Another plan was to lure him to a park and the Runner, dressed as a woman and pushing a pram, would walk past and shoot him. He and Williams bought a shoulder-length brown wig before abandoning the plan. Just as well. The Runner didn't have the legs to carry it off.

Killer? Yes. Drag queen? No.

But finding Moran proved more difficult than first believed. Moran was an expert in counter-surveillance and teamed with a man who appeared to be a bodyguard. He ditched his flamboyant lifestyle, rented a modest house in Moonee Ponds and kept on the move.

Also, the Runner had never met Moran and Williams did not provide him with a picture. Once the Runner saw a man matching the description leaving Moran's brother-in-law's home in Gladstone Park. 'I am pretty sure (it) was Jason.'

They finally spotted him in late February at a Red Rooster outlet in Gladstone Park. Williams was not armed. They followed him and an unidentified female who was driving a small black sedan.

As a surveillance operative Carl made a good drug dealer. He grabbed a tyre lever and a screwdriver from inside his car and followed at a distance of only twenty metres. According to the Runner, 'about 40 or 50 metres down this road (Johnson Street) the rear of the hatch of the car opened up and Jason shot several shots at us from the back of the car.'

Williams lost interest, saying, 'We will get him another time'.

Williams and the Runner went to pubs and clubs where they might find Moran. They may have ended up full but they came back empty. They thought about a hit at the Docks where Moran was said to occasionally work, but terrorist fears had resulted in a massive security upgrade that made it impossible.

Williams started to get desperate. If he couldn't get to Jason he would kill those close to him. He told the Runner to start surveillance on Moran's oldest family friend, Graham Kinniburgh, and another associate Steve (Fat Albert) Collins.

Kinniburgh was a legendary, semi-retired gangster, one of those rare, successful criminals hardly known outside police and underworld circles. But he was a close friend of Jason's father, Lewis Moran.

Williams then figured that even an erratic man like Moran must have a routine that centred on his family. He and Moran were linked by more than greed, drugs and hatred; their children went to the same private school in the Essendon area.

Williams finally put a bounty on Moran's head in April 2003. Veniamin and the Runner would get $100,000 each. The pair, armed and masked, hid in the back seat of a rented car outside the school expecting Jason to drop his children off. But he did not show. Later, Roberta Williams picked a fight with Jason's wife Trish outside the school in the hope she would call her husband to come to support her. Still no Jason.

Williams wanted Veniamin (who was still associating with Gatto and the Carlton Crew) to set up Moran for an ambush but Benji was frightened Big Mick would realise he was working for Williams.

'Carl was becoming wary of Andrew and told me that he was concerned that Andrew was more in the Moran camp than in ours,' the Runner later told police.

In fact, Williams believed Moran was trying to persuade Veniamin to become a double agent and kill Carl.

When Benji failed to deliver Moran to a planned ambush at the Spencer Street taxi rank near *The Age* building, Williams started to doubt his number one killer.

'From then on Carl would only meet Andrew on his own terms. That way Carl could be sure of his own safety. He did not trust Andrew any more,' the Runner said.

Certainly Williams was jumpy. An interstate AFL spy wanted to check out the Essendon team at Windy Hill but as it was a locked training session he drove to one end of the ground where he hoped to use his set of binoculars to learn about the opposition's game plan.

He lost interest in sport when Williams, whose mother lived nearby, fronted him, believing the spy was trying to follow him.

The spy waved a *Football Record* at him telling him his only interest in sharp-shooters was to judge the fitness of Essendon's star full-forward, Matthew Lloyd. The Williams team learned that Moran took his children to Auskick training every Saturday morning in Essendon North, near the Cross Keys Hotel. Williams had eased Veniamin out of the hit team and replaced him with the getaway driver from the Mark Moran murder.

The Runner and his new partner, the 'Driver', inspected the football oval and planned an ambush. On June 14, 2003, armed and ready, they watched the football clinic but did not see Jason. They agreed to try again the next week.

Williams had another plan. He wanted not only to kill Moran, but also to make a statement that no-one could mistake. He told the Runner he wanted Jason ambushed on June 15, the anniversary of Mark's murder at the grave-site at the Fawkner Cemetery.

'Carl decided though that if we were not able to kill Jason on Sunday (June 15) then we would try again at Auskick next week.'

It was too late to do the necessary homework and on the assigned day it took the hit team more than an hour to find the grave. By then the window of opportunity had shut. When they arrived they found a card signed by Jason. They had missed their mark, but only just. As they left they saw a car fly through a red light. It was probably Moran.

During the following week the team repeatedly went to the Cross Keys ground to fine-tune their planned hit. The Runner would be dropped at the hotel car park where Moran would be parked; he would run up, shoot Moran in the head and then run over a footbridge to the getaway van.

At the precise moment of the hit Williams was committed to spilling blood but in an environment far more sterile than the grubby murder scene. He organised a blood test for that morning, giving him an alibi he would need for the police.

On the Saturday morning they collected guns from the Pascoe

184

Vale house of Andrew Krakouer (brother to former footballers Jimmy and Phil), which Williams used as a safe house, and placed stolen plates on the white van that would be used in the getaway.

Williams' lieutenant, a man who could source chemicals for amphetamines and who cannot be named, then advised the Runner to 'get Jason good and get him in the head'.

The Lieutenant later disputed this when he became a police witness. He claimed he told the Driver to do the killing away from the kids at the Auskick – 'Hey, I'm no monster.'

They sat near the park when the Runner spotted a man he believed was the target. 'I thought it might have been Jason because people were coming up to him, shaking his hand and generally paying attention to him. His behaviour was typical of a gangster.'

Williams and the Lieutenant drove past and nodded to confirm they had seen the target then headed off for their blood tests – proving you can get blood from a stone killer.

As the clinic was about to wind up the hit team watched Moran head back to the hotel car park to hop in a blue van. Williams' men drove to the rear of the car park. 'I then put on my balaclava and gloves and jumped out from the van, carrying the shotgun in my right hand. I had the two revolvers in a belt around my waist. I ran to the driver's side window of the blue van, aimed the shotgun at Jason Moran and fired through the closed window.

Moran slumped forward and the Runner fired again. He dropped the shotgun, grabbed his long-barrelled revolver and fired at least another three shots. He then took off, running over the footbridge to the waiting van.

The other man in the blue van with Jason was Pasquale Barbaro, a small-time crook who worked for Moran. The Runner later said he didn't see Barbaro let alone intend to kill him. 'I did not even know that I had shot Pasquale Barbaro until later … I regret that happening.'

Williams received news of the hit with the message that 'the horse … had been scratched'.

Later, Williams and the Lieutenant congratulated the Runner on a 'job well done' and gave him $2500 cash. He was promised a unit in Frankston as payment but it failed to eventuate. The killer was short-changed and in business terms it would prove a short-sighted decision. But if it worried the hired gunman it didn't show; hours after killing two men and scrubbing off gunshot residue he attended a birthday party at a North Melbourne restaurant.

Murder, it would seem, can sharpen the appetite.

Another person was clearly pleased with the news of Moran's death. Roberta Williams was picked up on a bug shortly after the murders saying: 'I'll be partying tonight.'

# First breakthrough

EVEN though Williams was the obvious suspect his blood test alibi was standing up. The shotgun found at the scene had not been traced and those around the Williams camp said nothing.

There had been eleven underworld murders since 2000 and all remained unsolved. Police initially treated each crime individually, despite it being obvious that some (but not all) of the murders were connected.

Senior homicide investigator Phil Swindells was frustrated by the lack of results and began lobbying for a task force. He reported that Andrew Veniamin was suspected of three murders and a task force was necessary to target his group. Senior police finally acted and the Rimer task group (later renamed Purana) was established in May 2003, with Detective Senior Sergeant Swindells in charge.

Many believed it was doomed to fail. 'We had no intelligence and we didn't know anything about many of the major players,' Swindells recalled. Assistant Commissioner Simon Overland would later admit that police 'dropped the ball'.

Swindells knew there would be no early arrests and there might be more murders. He also knew police had to go back to the start and build up dossiers on all the players. Only then would they be able to try to isolate the weak links.

Politicians, self-proclaimed media experts and cynical old detectives thought Purana would self-destruct. A lack of success would result in bitter infighting and no results. The underworld code of silence would never be broken, they said.

To keep up morale during the years of investigation the task force called on Essendon coach and long-time AFL survivor Kevin Sheedy to motivate Purana investigators. Believe in yourselves and your team-mates and don't worry about the scoreboard, he said. Do the planning and the results will come.

In October 2003 the task force was enlarged to 53 staff, including nine investigative groups, with Detective Inspector Andrew Allen in charge. From the start no-one really doubted that Williams was behind the killing but there was no hard evidence. Several names were nominated as the shooter, including the Runner, but names without facts were of little use.

The initial homicide squad team was convinced the Runner was the gunman and had identified others who would later be shown to be part of Williams' hit squad.

The initial work of the homicide squad cannot be underestimated. But it was the better-resourced Purana team that was able to make a series of breakthroughs.

It was months before the first strong lead emerged from the double murder. Near the Cross Keys Hotel in Moreland Road is a public telephone and detectives eventually checked the calls made at the time of the murder.

On a long list a series of numbers stood out. On Friday, June 20, the day before the double murder, someone rang Williams' mobile phone from the telephone box. Roberta Williams' mobile had also been called, and then the Runner's. It was clear to police that one of the hit team was checking out the layout for the ambush planned for the following day.

But the next call on the list was not a known suspect. When police tracked down the man who received the call he told them he had been rung that day by a mate. That friend was the Driver. It did not take long to find out that the Driver was a thief, drug dealer and close friend of Williams. He sold speed and had a lucrative sideline in stolen Viagra. He was still selling the remains of 10,175 sample packs he stole from a Cheltenham warehouse in April 2000.

Detectives drove to the Driver's house. Sitting in the driveway was a white van, the same type as the one captured on closed circuit video depositing a masked gunman in the car park moments before Moran and Barbaro were killed.

It was a breakthrough – but not the breakthrough. It would take police fourteen months before they could lay charges. Meanwhile, the murders continued.

## Closing in

PURANA detectives knew that the Williams team would eventually make a mistake, but how many would die before they found the weak link?

In October 2003 police learned that the Driver, Williams' trusted associate, had sourced an abandoned sedan rebuilt by a backyard mechanic – a perfect getaway vehicle.

Police placed a listening device in the car and waited. But the Driver, having collected the car and driven it a short distance, noticed the brake light was on. He checked it, and found the bug, which he ripped out. He immediately told the Runner 'we're hot' and wanted to cancel the job. But the Runner had lost his sense of risk and suggested they push on.

'(The Driver) mentioned to me that he had found what he thought was a tracker in the car. I dismissed the thought because my mind was focussed on doing the job ... I decided to keep going without the clean car. In hindsight it was sheer stupidity that I didn't take notice of the locating of a tracking device, but my mind was elsewhere and I was feeling the pressure of the job and that we had already wasted enough time'.

That night they met Williams separately in Flemington for new instructions but Williams' growing sense of invincibility resulted in a massive misjudgment on his part. The one-time suburban drug dealer, with new-found ambitions of gangland domination, ordered his hit team to carry on.

Inexplicably the Driver decided to use his own car (a silver Holden Vectra sedan once owned by Williams) to drive to the scene. But it, too, was bugged with recording and tracking devices.

Police knew that the Runner and the Driver planned a major crime in a square kilometre block of South Yarra but did not know what that crime would be.

In the week before the major crime took place, the pair repeatedly drove around the block of Chapel Street and Malvern, Toorak and Williams roads. Police suspected the pair were planning an armed robbery and identified potential targets including the TAB at the Bush Inn Hotel and two luxury car dealers.

A week later, on Saturday October 25, the Purana chief, Detective Inspector Andrew Allen, was at work catching up on paperwork when he got a call from police monitoring the car.

The suspects had been talking about guns, getaways and something 'going down'. But the tracker failed (they drop out in the same manner as mobile phones) so police could not identify the car's location. Detectives could only sit back and listen as they still did not know the men's intended target. They could hear muffled gunshots and the suspects driving off. Police soon received calls that a man was lying in Joy Street, South Yarra. It was Michael Ronald Marshall, 38, drug dealer and nightclub hotdog salesman.

Marshall had just got out of his four-wheel-drive, his five-year-old son still in the vehicle. The Runner later told police that he shot the drug dealer four times in the street before escaping.

'I was jogging along the footpath towards Marshall's driver's side door as he hadn't got out yet. Just before I got to his car I pulled the balaclava down over my face. I was about three metres away from the driver's door, standing in the middle of the road when Marshall started to get out of the car.

'I had the gun in my right hand and Marshall was out of the car and noticed me. We looked at each other briefly and I started to raise the gun as he went to lunge at me. As he lunged I fired a shot but I am unsure if this hit him. As the gun fired, the kickback, along with the combination of me taking a step backwards from Marshall's lunge caused me to fall over. I also think the ground may have been a bit wet. I quickly got up again and was face to face with Marshall. He was a large person, over six feet tall and I was aware he was a former kickboxer.

'I was concerned that he might overpower me so I just began firing shots at him at close range to the head area. I am not sure how many shots I fired; I think it may have been three or four. Marshall started to fall to the ground and I think I fired one more shot into his head as he was going down towards my feet. At no stage during the altercation did I see or realise that Marshall's son was still with him.'

On the way back the Driver said to the Runner: 'Should I ring the Big Fella?' Later the Runner rang Williams to tell him, again, 'that horse has just been scratched'.

Again they were stupid. The Driver had found a police listening device in his house but decided to leave it there – working on the basis that if he knew its location he would avoid making incriminating statements within its range.

Perhaps he forgot but the 'scratched' comment was made around 5pm – after the last race of the day. Williams just grunted when told – but it was enough.

Within hours the Runner and the Driver were arrested. The walls were starting to close in on the Premier.

Police knew who killed Marshall and who ordered the hit, but it would be more than two years before they learned why. And it would support their long-held theory that behind the scenes millionaire drug dealer Tony Mokbel was attempting to pull the strings.

## The murders continue

ON December 22, 2003, Williams and Andrew Veniamin met Mick Gatto at the Crown Casino in what were supposed to be peace talks. It was only days after Gatto's close friend, Graham Kinniburgh, had been gunned down outside his Kew home.

Kinniburgh was an old-time gangster who made his name as Australia's best safebreaker. For three decades he has been connected with some of Australia's biggest crimes. Police say he was the mastermind behind the magnetic drill gang – Australia's best safe-breaking crew – that grabbed $1.7 million from a NSW bank, a huge jewellery haul from a Lonsdale Street office and valuables from safety deposit boxes in Melbourne.

He had put his children through private school and was semi-retired but he was also a friend of Jason Moran's father, Lewis, and therefore Williams saw him as an enemy.

Kinniburgh was a man who rarely smiled but in his final few months he became morose. The keen punter and expert numbers man could read the play and knew there would be an attempt on his life. He began to carry a gun and told a friend: 'My card has been marked'. He was shot dead on December 13, 2003, while carrying his shopping from his car to his house.

Williams told the author 36 hours after the murder that he was not involved: 'I've never met him and I've never heard a bad thing said about him. I have nothing to profit from his death. It's a mystery to me. I haven't done anything. My conscience is clear.'

Nine days after the murder Williams and Andrew Veniamin met Mick Gatto at the Crown Casino. It was an open secret that Gatto was on Williams' death list and this was seen as the last chance to stop the killings.

'If anything comes my way then I'll send somebody to you. I'll be careful with you, be careful with me,' Gatto warned. 'I believe you, you believe me, now we're even. That's a warning,' he said. 'It's not my war.'

For perhaps the first time Williams wavered. He went to see the Lieutenant for a second opinion. Should he trust Mick and declare a truce?

The Lieutenant said: 'Ask Benji. He knows him (Gatto) better than me.' Williams already had and Veniamin had no doubts. 'Kill him,' was his answer. Veniamin effectively passed his own death sentence.

Gatto shot Veniamin dead in a Carlton restaurant on March 23, 2004. Gatto was acquitted of murder on the grounds of self-defence by a Supreme Court jury in June 2005.

Eight days after Veniamin died, Williams hit back.

Lewis Moran was shattered by the death of his stepson Mark

and his natural son Jason. But it was the death of his best friend, Kinniburgh, that destroyed his will to live. Someone who had known him for years said 'Lewis loved money. He was rich but he didn't know how to have a good time.'

He was introduced to the drug business by his sons and embraced the wealth it generated. Friends said he liked to watch cooking shows during the day, do a little business in the late afternoon and drink from about 6pm. He was notorious for hiding money, much of which has never been found.

Once he hid $14,000 in an oven and was shattered when someone turned it on – shrinking the notes to the size of Monopoly money. But there was a happy ending. Kinniburgh found a compliant bank manager in Sydney who would accept the cash.

Lewis, a former skilled pickpocket, tried to carry a gun after Mark and Jason were murdered but arthritis made him more a danger to himself. Once when he tried to load the handgun he fired a shot through the floor of a car.

Moran had little formal education but, as an experienced SP bookmaker, he was gifted when it came to numbers. He could calculate odds in a flash and after Kinniburgh was murdered he knew his own survival was a long shot.

When he was bailed on drug charges he saw his former lawyer, Andrew Fraser, who was in the same prison serving five years over his own drug conviction. Fraser said he'd see him later. Moran shook his head and said he wouldn't. He knew what was around the darkened corner.

Williams denied the existence of a death list and told the author: 'I've only met Lewis once. I haven't got a problem with Lewis. If he thinks he has a problem with me I can say he can sleep peacefully.'

Not only was Williams a murderer but he was also, it would seem, a terrible fibber.

Police knew Moran was a sitting duck and they successfully applied to have a court-ordered bail curfew altered so his movements would not be easily anticipated by would-be hitmen.

Detective Senior Sergeant Swindells gave evidence in the forlorn hope he could save Moran's life.

He said Moran's 'vulnerability relates to a perception by the task force that if the curfew remains between 8pm and 8am ... it is possible for any person to be lying in wait for Mr Moran to return to his home address'.

But Lewis no longer cared. He knew that if he stuck to a routine he was more vulnerable but he continued to drink at the Brunswick Club – where he was shot dead by two contract killers on March 31, 2004. The killers were allegedly paid $140,000 cash (it is doubtful they declared the GST component). They were supposed to be paid $150,000 but were short-changed.

As a friend said, 'Lewis died because he loved cheap beer.'

# The false dawn

POLICE knew they needed a circuit breaker and this would best be achieved by jailing Williams. And it was the Premier himself, always so cautious about phones, who handed them the damning evidence. He told his wife in one call that if Purana Detective Sergeant Stuart Bateson raided their house she should 'grab the gun from under the mattress and shoot them in the head'.

In a prison phone call the Runner complained of his treatment and Williams talked about chopping up Sergeant Bateson's girlfriend.

Bateson was not a policeman to be intimidated. He received the Valour Award in 1991 after he wrestled a gunman to the ground and disarmed him after the offender had forced another policeman to his knees at gunpoint.

The tape of Williams' threats was the break police needed and on November 17, 2003, the Special Operations Group grabbed Williams in Beaconsfield Parade, Port Melbourne.

The arrest, captured by *The Age's* photographer Angela Wylie, was the image of the man who thought he was beyond the law lying helplessly on the ground with detectives standing over him. It was a sign that the times were changing.

Purana police believed they had enough to hold him but he was bailed for a third time. On the outside police suspect he was able to organise at least another three murders.

In the two weeks before he was bailed, Williams befriended another would-be tough-guy in prison who was keen to be fast-tracked. He was an alleged heroin trafficker and amateur boxer with a big mouth who would finally bring the big man down.

## Needle in a haystack

ONE of the most boring jobs in a long investigation is to monitor police bugging devices. The Purana task force virtually dominated the technical capacity of the entire crime department with many detectives in other areas quietly grumbling that their investigations were put on hold after Simon Overland ordered the gangland detectives were to be given priority.

During the investigation Purana would log a staggering 500,000 telephone conversations – most of them consisting of the inarticulate ramblings of would-be-gangsters. They used listening devices to bug suspects for 53,000 hours and conducted 22,000 hours of physical surveillance.

Police on the case found that listening to the Williams family was cruel and unusual punishment. 'It was like being subjected to the *Jerry Springer Show* 24 hours a day,' one said.

At one stage Roberta was talking to Carl when the son from her previous marriage distracted her. 'Put it down,' she said, and then told Carl in a matter-of-fact voice what 'it' was. 'He's got the tomahawk,' she said.

In another conversation she was talking to Greg Domaszewicz, the babysitter accused of killing little Jaidyn Leskie who died in Moe in 1997.

Roberta was complaining how difficult it was to look after the children when Carl was in prison. Domaszewicz suggested he could pop around and look after them if she needed a break. After a pause she responded to the offer. 'You're fucking joking aren't you?'

Carl Williams always assumed his phone, house and cars were bugged. When he wanted a business discussion he chose open parks or noisy fast food restaurants. This also suited his appetite as the big bloke had a weakness for chicken and chips.

For police trying to trap the Williams crew through bugging operations was like trying to find a needle in a haystack.

But in late May 2004 they found it. Two of Williams' soldiers sat in what they thought was a clean car and discussed their plan to kill a close friend of Mick Gatto and key member of the so-called Carlton Crew, Mario Condello.

The two men in the car reminded each other of the importance of their mission. 'We're not just doing a burg,' one said to the other.

Williams saw Condello as the money man of the team he was determined to destroy. He also thought the former lawyer turned gangster would find the money to take out a contract on him if he did not move first.

Condello and Gatto were close, so close that when Big Mick was in jail waiting for his trial over the Veniamin killing he asked Mario to keep an eye on business.

He also advised Condello, 'Keep your eyes wide opened; you

can't trust any of these rats. I would hate to see anything happen to any of ours.'

The Williams' team had done their homework. They knew Condello was a creature of habit and took his small dog for an early morning walk past the Brighton Cemetery most weekdays.

It was the perfect place for an ambush. Police agreed, but their plan was to ambush the hit team before they could strike.

It was the beginning of a secret police high-risk, high-reward operation, codenamed Lemma. Detective Inspector Gavan Ryan was in charge of the 170 police needed to surround the area without spooking the hitmen.

The would-be killers may have been committed but they weren't punctual.

Twice when they were supposed to kill Condello they simply slept in. The second time one of the team had chatted up a woman and preferred a hot one-night stand to a cold-blooded early morning killing.

Finally they moved but were still using the car police had bugged and detectives could hear them preparing for the murder. But police also knew Condello had left the family home and moved into a city apartment. He also had heard he was on the hit list and moved out of his house to try to protect his family.

But then Ryan heard one of the team spot a big man walking his small dog near the cemetery.

One of the gunman was clearly heard asking, 'Is that the man, is that the man?'

Incredibly, another local with a similar build to Condello was walking a small dog on exactly the same route.

'He shouldn't bother buying Tattslotto tickets. I think he used all his luck that morning,' the Director of Public Prosecutions, Paul Coghlan, said.

With the would-be hitmen becoming jumpy Ryan knew it was time to move.

Police arrested two men at the scene. They also seized two pistols, two-way radios and a stolen getaway car.

They then arrested Williams at his mother's home in Primrose Street, Essendon and Williams' cousin Michael Thorneycroft in an outer eastern suburb.

Thorneycroft would later tell police he was offered $30,000 to be the driver for the hit team and the shooter stood to make $120,000.

For police it was a major breakthrough. But for Mario Condello it was only to be a delay. After the attempt on his life he was interviewed on Channel Nine and publicly addressed the Williams' team: 'My message is stay away from me. I'm bad luck to you people. Stay away. Don't come near me please.'

He also expressed a poetic wish that the violence stop 'and everything becomes more peaceful than it has over the last however many years, because after all we are not going to be here forever.'

He was right.

Mario Condello was shot dead as he returned to his East Brighton home on February 6, 2006. He was on bail charged with, among other things, incitement to murder Carl Williams.

But the arrest of the hit team outside the Brighton Cemetery was the beginning of the end of Melbourne's underworld war. It meant that after five years of trying police were finally able to put Williams inside jail on charges that guaranteed he would not be bailed.

According to Ryan the arrest of the hit team was the moment that police finally seized the initiative – four years after Williams declared war with the murder of Mark Moran. 'For us (Operation Lemma) it was the turning point. It was the first time we were in front of the game.'

# The mutiny

CARL Williams had previously done jail time easily. But this time he was in the highest security rating and locked up for 23 hours a day. In one video link to court his lawyers argued that Williams had not been able to hold or touch his young daughter since his placement in maximum security.

No-one mentioned the feelings of the children of the men he murdered in the previous five years.

Williams knew he was in trouble. He knew some of his troops were starting to waver and the so-called wall of silence was starting to crack. He started to threaten and cajole members of his team to stay staunch, working on those he thought were the most susceptible.

But he always assumed that the Runner, the career armed robber and willing killer, was unbreakable.

This was a man who had never co-operated with police. When forensic experts took a swab from his gums in prison after the Marshall murder they were horrified to find a 'brown substance' in his mouth. The substance, designed to compromise the test, was not identified. But it was definitely not breath freshener.

The case against the Runner was compelling. Marshall's blood was found on his pants and police had the bugged conversations and positive identifications.

At first the Runner wanted to fight. On the advice of his lawyer the fit-looking Runner put on 30 kilograms to try to beat eyewitness descriptions, and he wanted Williams to fund a Queen's Counsel for his case.

But Williams knew the Runner was doomed and decided to cut him free so Williams could save himself. He wanted his loyal soldier to plead guilty and cop a life sentence. The cash flow stopped and the Runner was left to the mercy of legal aid while his boss continued to employ the best lawyers money could buy.

Williams didn't want to be sitting in the criminal dock with the Runner as the evidence was put to a jury. He believed he still stood a chance if he managed to get a separate trial.

But in early 2006 Crown Prosecutor Geoff Horgan, SC, returned from his summer break to find a letter from prison. It was the Runner and he wanted to talk. The note was non-committal but the message was clear. The soldier was ready for mutiny.

'To us it was unbelievable. He was seen as one of the hardest men in the system,' Horgan said.

Ryan, who was by then the head of Purana, went to see the Runner. 'He didn't need persuading, he was ready to talk. None of us imagined he would roll over.'

The Runner was removed from prison and for nearly 30 days exposed the secrets of Melbourne's gangland murders, sinking any hopes for Williams in the process.

Inspector Ryan, Detective Sergeant Stuart Bateson, and senior detectives Nigel L'estrange, Mark Hatt and Michelle Kelly questioned him for weeks. A stream of Purana detectives questioned him on individual murders.

Police guarded him, fed him and did his washing as he exposed all Williams' dirty laundry.

He told them about the crimes they knew he had committed but implicated himself in ones they didn't.

He told them he was the driver in the two-man hit team assigned to kill drug dealer and standover man Nik 'The Bulgarian' Radev, who was shot dead in Coburg on April 15, 2003.

Radev was a violent gangster who desperately wanted to meet the amphetamine expert who produced drugs for Williams and another well-known dealer. But Williams knew that if Radev discovered the identity of their production expert he would abduct and torture him to persuade the self-tutored drug chemist to become an exclusive Radev employee.

That morning Radev was told at a meeting in Brighton that he would finally meet the chemist across town in Queen Street, Coburg. According to the Runner, 'I drove Veniamin to murder Nik Radev'.

As five of Williams' closest allies turned on him and became police witnesses Purana discovered more about the crimes of the Premier.

They found that Williams had offered the contract to kill Jason Moran to others, including notorious killer, drug dealer and armed robber Victor George Peirce who was shot dead in Bay Street, Port Melbourne on May 1, 2002.

Peirce was paid $100,000 in advance and was to pocket a further $100,000 on completion when he killed Moran. But Peirce changed sides and warned Moran.

Another career criminal was shot after he refused to carry out a contract to kill Moran. Convicted murderer Mark Anthony Smith supposedly agreed and then refused to kill Moran. So Smith was shot in the neck in the driveway of his Keilor home on December 28, 2002. He recovered and fled to Queensland for several months.

So was Peirce killed because he refused to kill Moran? The trouble with criminals like Victor Peirce is they always have more than one set of enemies who want to see them dead.

His best friend was Frank Benvenuto, son of the late Godfather of Melbourne, Liborio. Peirce had worked in the fruit and vegetable market for Frank Benvenuto during a major power struggle in the business.

Peirce was not there to lug turnips. He once arrived at work armed with a machine-gun.

But for Frank, having Peirce on his side was not enough. On

May 8, 2000, Benvenuto was shot dead outside his Beaumaris home. The shooter was Andrew Veniamin. But who paid for the hit and why?

Veniamin knew that Peirce suspected he was the gunman. The two killers met to try to establish a truce.

According to Victor's widow, Wendy, 'They met in a Port Melbourne park. He wanted to know if Victor was going to back up for Frank.'

According to Mrs Peirce her husband assured Veniamin there would be no payback.

Benji was not convinced.

Police say Veniamin was the gunman who shot Peirce in Port Melbourne and while Benji worked for Williams he also did freelance work.

So while Williams had reasons to detest Peirce for not carrying out the contract on Moran, Veniamin had his own reasons to want the target dead.

And whoever paid Veniamin to kill Benvenuto would also have been relieved when Peirce was no longer a living threat.

Jason Moran was a prominent mourner at Peirce's funeral. The next year he would also be shot dead.

# Deals within deals

FOR Purana investigators to crack the underworld code of silence they needed to offer deals that were too good to refuse. In doing so they have changed the model of plea bargaining in Victoria forever.

Purana police previously refused to do deals with trigger men but senior police and legal strategists in the Office of Public Prosecutions decided it was more important to nail the underworld generals who ordered the killings than the soldiers who carried them out.

# BOYS WITH TOYS

From early in the investigation police had two main targets, Carl Williams and Tony Mokbel. One they knew was behind the killings and the other they suspected.

Paid killers can expect life in prison with no chance of release. Their crimes are not based on passion or psychological problems but greed.

But under the Purana model some of Melbourne's worst gangsters were offered a chance of freedom if they turned on Williams and Mokbel.

Men who had spent decades in jail and had never talked were courted. By now they were middle-aged and the thought of never being released was too much for them to contemplate.

The Purana task force used the proven US tactic of turning alleged hitmen into star witnesses. The most notorious was Salvatore 'Sammy the Bull' Gravano, a former underboss of the New York Gambino family.

The first to do a deal was the Driver. He was sentenced to eighteen years with a minimum of ten for his role in the murder of Michael Marshall and he was never charged with his involvement in the killings of Mark Moran, Jason Moran and Pasquale Barbaro.

It was a dream deal for a man who could have faced a life sentence but he was the domino who made the others fall.

'Without him we wouldn't have been able to move on Cross Keys (Jason Moran and Pasquale Barbaro),' Horgan said.

But it was the confessions of the Runner that finally tipped the balance – implicating Williams in six murders and exposing Mokbel's alleged role in the underworld war.

The Runner was moved from his prison in Victoria and is believed to be interstate. He was sentenced to a minimum of 23 years for the murders of Marshall, Jason Moran and Pasquale Moran. He will be in his early 70s when he becomes eligible for release.

Police were confident they could make a case against Mokbel for murder. So, it would seem, was Mokbel.

Days before he was found guilty of cocaine trafficking in March 2006 Mokbel jumped bail and disappeared overseas. But police say it was not the fact that he would be sentenced to a manageable term (a minimum of nine years) for drug trafficking that made him run.

In the week before he disappeared a lawyer gave him the Runner's secret statements and Mokbel knew he was likely to be charged with murder.

On March 20, he fled. But the Purana task force was always confident he would surface and began to dismantle his financial empire.

In February 2007, Mokbel was charged with Lewis Moran's murder.

In June he (and the bad wig he was wearing) was arrested in Greece and a few weeks later was charged with the murder of Michael Marshall. Despite his high-profile drug convictions and his decision to jump bail juries will judge his guilt or innocence on the fresh charges at a later date.

Once the Runner made his statements Williams knew there was no chance he could beat the mounting charges. Williams was convicted of the Marshall murder and sentenced to a minimum of 21 years.

The verdict was suppressed because he had multiple trials pending, including the murders of Mark Moran and the murders of Jason Moran and Pasquale Barbaro.

For months Williams was secretly trying to negotiate a deal that gave him some chance of release and in February 2007, on the eve of his trial for the murders of Jason Moran and Barbaro, he finally pleaded guilty.

It was around August 2006 that the man who once had teams of hitmen prepared to kill for him knew he was facing the rest of his life in jail. Several of his trusted offsiders had cut deals with prosecutors leaving him increasingly isolated.

He knew if he pleaded guilty he would be entitled to a discount. Aged 35 he wanted a chance to be out of jail by the age of 70.

But the first tentative approaches were not encouraging. His team floated a prison sentence of around twelve years. 'They were looking for a ridiculous bargain-basement sentence,' said Paul Coghlan, QC.

But as the trial date came closer so too did the negotiators. In February the two sides spent ten days talking. Then what had appeared promising collapsed.

According to Coghlan. 'We were very cross. We thought Williams had been fooling around and was never serious. He was wasting our time because they came up with various proposals that were absolutely laughable.'

On Wednesday February 28 at midday the court process began before Justice King with pre-trial discussions.

It was legal tent-boxing with a few slow punches thrown without any landing.

First Williams' team asked for an adjournment because of pre-trial publicity but the same argument had been tried before and failed.

Next was a move to suggest there was judicial bias – another move doomed to fail.

Then it was agreed the star protected witnesses could give video evidence for security reasons. By 1pm the court was adjourned for the day.

There would be a few more pre-trial details to be cleared up and then a jury would be selected.

On Monday, March 5, Geoff Horgan was scheduled to rise to his feet to begin his opening address to declare that Williams organised the murders of Jason Moran and Pasquale Barbaro, who were shot dead on June 21, 2003, while watching an Auskick junior football clinic.

Once the jury was empanelled any chance of a deal for Williams would be over.

It was 2.10pm on February 28 when Horgan received a call in his chambers from Williams' barrister, David Ross, QC. The message was brief: 'We may have a deal.'

A message was passed to Justice King's associate Helen Marriott and a decision made to reconvene the court that day.

But Williams had left the court and was heading down the Princes Freeway to Barwon Prison. Then Justice King intervened and ordered the bus back.

This was no sweetheart deal. The prosecutors agreed they would make no recommendations on a jail sentence although they acknowledge Williams should be set a minimum due to his decision to plead. 'His sentence will be totally up to the judge,' Horgan said.

The charge sheet was quickly typed, documents signed and Williams led back into court.

But the crime deal of the decade that resulted in Williams pleading guilty to three murders was teetering on the point of collapse when Justice Betty King reconvened her court after being told of his decision.

While it took nearly seven months of secret negotiations to bring Williams to the point where he was prepared to admit his guilt the final deal was nearly derailed in the final minutes.

The man linked to ten underworld killings had just told his relieved lawyers he would plead to the murders of Lewis Moran, Jason Moran and Mark Mallia and conspiracy to murder Mario Condello. (He did not plead over Barbaro, arguing he had not ordered his death and the victim was killed accidentally. The Mark Moran murder charge was dropped.)

But his agreement was worth nothing. He had to say the

words 'I plead guilty' when his presentments were read to him in the open court.

Backroom deals don't count.

He had been brought up from the court cells to sign a document instructing his defence team of his intentions to enter guilty pleas.

Outside the court members of the police Purana task force stood waiting. One nervously said, 'I won't believe it until I hear him say it.'

Williams' mother, Barbara, and father, George, were also there and were then allowed in to see their son before the hearing commenced. While George remained quiet, Barbara was animated.

She pleaded with her son not to plead.

George didn't apply any pressure. Still facing drug trafficking charges, part of the deal was that Williams Senior would plead guilty but the prosecution would not demand a jail sentence.

According to an insider Carl began to waver as his mother begged him to change his mind.

The observer said the deal was 'within a hair's breadth' of collapsing. 'If we had lost him then maybe we would have lost him forever.'

But the court convened in front of Justice King and three times Williams admitted his guilt.

Then despite his mother's concern Williams nodded his head, a decision, Coghlan said, that saved millions of dollars and sent a message to the underworld that no-one is above the law.

Before Williams would agree to any deal he wanted to pass a message to a man on the outside. He desperately wanted him to know that no matter what, he wished him no harm. That man was Mick Gatto.

# Postscript

THE Runner, the Lieutenant and the Driver cannot be identified by name as they have been given protected witness status. All are in jail.

WILLIAMS' cousin, Michael Thorneycroft, 32, also became a protected witness but he couldn't grasp his second chance in life. He was the first to turn on Williams and tell police he was prepared to give evidence against him.

He was arrested with three others on June 9, 2004, and charged with conspiracy to murder former lawyer and gangland identity Mario Condello.

Soon after he turned against Williams, agreeing to plead guilty and make a prosecution statement. In return he was given a three-year suspended sentence.

He was offered a new identity but decided to live with his mother in Melbourne's east and although he was given a new name he always knew that Williams could have reached out if he wished.

Police urged him to move and start a new life but he told them he was determined to stay in the area where he lived but maintain a low profile.

He sought and received assurances from a relative of Williams that there would be no payback.

Thorneycroft returned to playing suburban football under his new name but began to lose his battle with drug addiction.

He was found dead in his Boronia home in May 2007 of a suspected drug overdose. Police say there were no suspicious circumstances.

PHIL Swindells has been promoted to Inspector and works in the Ethical Standards Department. Andrew Allen was promoted to Superintendent and is in charge of the Geelong district. Gavan Ryan is a Detective Inspector in charge of task force 400 and in 2007 was awarded the prestigious Australia Police Medal in the Queen's Birthday Honours.

Stuart Bateson was promoted to work as a crime strategy expert and Assistant Commissioner Simon Overland was promoted to Deputy Commissioner.

MEMBERS of the Purana task force, initial homicide investigators, Special Operations Group, bugging experts and surveillance police received commendation awards from Chief Commissioner Christine Nixon at a private dinner in 2006.

Ryan sang a duet with Chief Commissioner Nixon and the police showband at the function proving beyond reasonable doubt he is a better detective than nightclub crooner.

MICK Gatto lost 30 kilograms while in jail. On his release he put the weight back on and runs his successful crane company. He has been painted for the Archibald Prize.

ROBERTA Williams split from Carl Williams and was seeing someone else. She says she considered converting to Islam and was dubbed for a short time Roberka. Carl Williams' new girlfriend was in court to see him plead guilty. Wearing a new engagement ring she is called a 'glass-widow' – a woman who visits her partner in prison but never has to touch him, although taped prison phone calls indicate their conversations can be quite risqué.

# CHAPTER 10

# A fatal miscalculation

'You are a killer, and a cowardly one who employed others to do the actual killing.'

CARL Williams spent years successfully avoiding an assassin's bullet only to commit legal suicide while giving evidence in the days leading to his final sentencing in the Supreme Court.

Stubborn to the end, the baby-faced killer turned his back on a sweet legal deal by ignoring his lawyer's advice to shut up and at least pretend to be sorry for launching a bloody vendetta that cost more than a dozen lives.

Williams was found guilty by a jury of the murder of Michael Marshall in October 2003.

When he finally realised that the prosecution case was overwhelming, he pleaded guilty to the murders of Jason Moran (June 2003), Mark Mallia (August 2003) and Lewis Moran (March 2004). He also pleaded guilty to the 2004 conspiracy to murder Mario Condello.

In agreeing to plead guilty, Williams cut a deal that literally meant he got away with murder – many times.

He also killed or was connected to those who killed Mark

Moran (June 2000), 'Mad Richard' Mladenich (May 2000), Willie Thompson (July 2003), Nik Radev (April 2003) and Victor Peirce (May 2002). He was directly responsible for the death of Pasquale Barbaro, who was accidentally shot dead by one of Williams' hitmen while murdering Jason Moran.

Williams is also suspected of ordering the murder of Graeme Kinniburgh, who was shot dead outside his Kew home in December 2003, and has been linked to several more gangland killings.

Paranoid, frightened and self-deluded, he survived and prospered by surrounding himself with a gang of soldiers whose loyalty he won with a combination of drugs, money, power and women.

But once he was inside jail, trusted subordinates began to waver. One by one they broke the code of silence and became prosecution witnesses.

Key members of the Williams' camp crossed the floor leaving the man who called himself 'The Premier' (boasting 'I run this state') without the numbers to survive.

So why then did the prosecution accept a plea and do a deal with the multiple killer? Why didn't it convict him again and again for the murders he committed?

Because it would have taken up to ten years and cost millions of dollars.

It would also have given Williams the public platform and the media attention he craved. By locking him away it condemns him to – as he has declared himself – a life of 'Groundhog Day'. As it was to turn out – 12,783 of them.

Williams first made noises that he might be prepared to do a deal as early as November 2006. He implied he had information that could help crack the murders of police informer Terence Hodson and his wife Christine, who were shot dead in their Kew home in May 2004.

# A FATAL MISCALCULATION

Detectives believe rogue police were responsible for the double murder, so if Williams could provide information he would have been able to demand a savage discount on his sentence.

But he was teasing. Williams did end up making a statement to police, but it was of little real value.

During the long pre-trial process before Williams was due to face the court for murdering Jason Moran and Pasquale Barbaro, his lawyers asked Justice Betty King: If he pleaded guilty, would the sentence be 'crushing'?

While no promises were made, they were told Williams could expect to see some light at the end of the tunnel.

Justice King is no bleeding heart. She is a commonsense judge who simply made her ruling on the basis of hard legal precedent.

The former hard-hitting prosecutor and senior member of the National Crime Authority was well aware of the case law surrounding guilty pleas.

Paul Charles Denyer is a serial killer who stalked and murdered three women in Frankston in 1993.

He pleaded guilty and was sentenced to life with no minimum by Supreme Court Justice Frank Vincent, but on appeal he was given a minimum of 30 years on the grounds that he should receive a discount for his guilty plea – no matter how reprehensible his crimes.

Leslie Alfred Camilleri, who killed two Bega schoolgirls in 1997, pleaded not guilty and was given life with no minimum. His partner, Lindsay Hoani Beckett, pleaded guilty and received a minimum of 35 years.

Justice King knew that if Williams pleaded she would be required to set a minimum sentence. The maximum of life was never in doubt.

Williams said he wanted a sentence that would give him some

chance of getting out by the age of 70. Purana Task Force police said they would push for a lighter sentence if he was prepared to become a witness in subsequent trials.

They wanted him to turn on his former role model, multi-millionaire drug boss Tony Mokbel, who fled Australia in March 2006 only to be recaptured in Greece in June the following year.

Mokbel allegedly paid Williams to organise the murder of Michael Marshall and police claimed he was also linked to the murder of Lewis Moran.

They wanted Williams to become a star prosecution witness.

While Williams may be many things, he remains an old-school crook who believes in the code of silence. And while many of Williams' old pals turned on him he remained determined to stay staunch.

After he decided to plead guilty he pretended to co-operate but anything he said was carefully crafted to lack real evidentiary value.

He made sure no-one would do jail time on the basis of what he said.

So without a promise to become a Crown witness, Williams' negotiating position was weakened. The final deal struck was that prosecutors would not demand a crushing sentence and would not oppose a move for Williams' father, George, to receive a suspended sentence for pending drug charges.

In effect, sentencing was to be left to Justice King without the prosecution lobbying for the longest jail term possible.

When Williams finally agreed to the deal on February 28, 2007 – just days before the jury was to be selected – the prison van taking him back to jail was called back so the papers could be signed and the plea formally entered before he changed his mind again.

In the minutes before the court was convened, his mother,

Barbara, urged him to abandon the deal and take his chances before a jury.

He would have been stupid to listen.

With the open and shut case against him, it was virtually certain he would have been convicted and given life with no minimum. George, whose own legal fate rested on his son's decision to plead, remained silent.

Once he pleaded, the rest should have been easy. He was to attend court for a public showing of mea culpa. He was to sit behind glass with a sad face and moo-cow eyes while his lawyers said how sorry he was.

They would say he thought the Moran family was out to kill him; that he would leave jail as an old man and would miss seeing his daughter Dhakota grow into an adult; and that he should receive a hefty discount because of his remorse.

But, against legal advice, Carl Williams insisted on giving evidence. The move was so stupid that his own legal team made him sign a waiver that he was doing it contrary to their expert opinion.

For almost an hour he gave ridiculous testimony contradicting known facts. He denied ever being paid money for the Marshall hit by Mokbel and tried to discredit Crown witnesses who were to give evidence against some of his mates.

Perhaps Williams' attempt to protect Mokbel was motivated by more than Aussie mateship.

The runaway drug boss had been paying his daughter's private school fees after Williams was locked up.

He also knew that when Mokbel was caught the convicted drug dealer would still be a major influence in the prison system. Carl knew Mokbel could be a good friend and a bad enemy.

Williams' testimony could not remain unchallenged. In the 90-minute cross-examination, prosecutor Geoff Horgan, SC, filleted Williams to protect the integrity of future Crown cases. Certainly Justice King questioned whether Williams was showing any remorse for his actions.

Williams left the court smiling.

His lawyers weren't. But the self-confessed killer was fully aware that his two hours in the sun would probably cost him another two years in a dark cell. He told friends later he was 'proud' of his performance.

He wanted his fellow prisoners to know he didn't dob anyone in to save himself.

Williams is not a stupid man. A psychiatric report declares him of 'high average intelligence'. He is not mentally ill. The report declares him to be broadly normal.

He was educated to Year 11 at Broadmeadows West Technical School and had a series of short-term labouring jobs before being employed as a supermarket packer. He acquired a minor criminal record but soon aimed higher – by 1994 he had embarked on a career as a full-time drug dealer.

By the time he married Roberta in January 2001 he had dreams of dominating the underworld.

He plotted revenge against the Morans after he was shot and then felt he had to keep killing anyone connected with them to remain alive. It was always going to end with him dead or in jail for most of his life.

So where to for Williams, who at 36 can only hope he lives long enough to be released as an old man?

After the brief excitement of the sentencing he returned to the maximum security Acacia Unit in Barwon prison where he socialises with a few loyal henchmen.

The minimum sentence will help prison officers control him. If he behaves badly in jail his eventual parole would be threatened leaving him facing life in jail.

Prison officers say indefinite sentences destroy inmates

because the dream of release is taken from them. Eventually, when threats die down, Williams will be transferred to the mainstream and if he behaves, he will eventually move to a more comfortable jail.

But he will always be a name. As he gets older and physically weaker he will become a target.

Even the toughest long-term inmates end up at risk of being bashed or stabbed.

Some time in the future, a violent young offender may attack him just for the bragging rights.

As the years pass, he will become institutionalised. His wife Roberta will have moved on (several times), his parents will have passed away, his daughter grown up and the glamorous blonde Renata Laureano, who pops in to jail to visit him, will have found a life.

Carl Williams may have got away with murder but there is one thing no one can beat – time. It eventually wounds all heels.

# The final curtain

DURING underworld murder hearings in Melbourne's Supreme Court we saw many sides of the respected Justice Betty King. We saw compassionate Betty, scholarly Betty and stern Betty. But for underworld killer Carl Williams when he was finally sentenced on May 7, 2007 it was definitely Ugly Betty.

Justice King had clearly had enough of Williams, who sat behind bulletproof glass looking by turn relaxed and bored as he listened to the reasons why he could not be released from jail until he was a pensioner.

Williams still hoped for a minimum sentence of around 33 years in exchange for his guilty plea, so he would be released before his 70th birthday.

He was being optimistic. His evidence during his plea hearing was so clearly bogus that any chance of that discount collapsed.

Purana Task Force police believe the no-nonsense Justice King had no choice but to revise her sentence upwards by at least two years after he showed no signs of remorse.

At law, a guilty plea is rewarded with a discounted sentence, and that discount can be increased through the accused showing sincere regret.

When addressing Williams as she sentenced him to life with a minimum non-parole period of 35 years, she said: 'I find that the evidence that you gave in the main was unbelievable, even incredible at times ... I find that the manner in which you gave evidence was arrogant, almost supercilious and you left me with a strong impression that your view of these murders was that they were all really justifiable and you were the real victim.

'You are a killer, and a cowardly one, who employed others to do the actual killing ... you should not be the subject of admiration by any member of our community.

'You were indeed the puppet master, deciding and controlling whether people lived or died.'

Minutes before the court convened Williams showed no sign that he understood that he was about to lose the best remaining years of his life.

He laughed and chatted with his mother, Barbara, who sat in the back row with Williams' father, George, and Carl's blonde friend, Renata Laureano.

It was as if Mrs Williams was farewelling her son on a ten-day Mediterranean cruise rather than three decades down the river. She will never see her son as a free man again.

A press photographer was given access to take a picture of Williams behind the glass. He smiled as if he had just won the blue ribbon for growing the biggest pumpkin at the Show.

As he sat flanked by seven big security guards, the woman

whose family he destroyed stared at him. Williams was pleading guilty to killing Judy Moran's son, Jason and husband, Lewis.

He had faced a charge of killing her other son, Mark, but it was dropped in exchange for his guilty plea.

Mrs Moran stood and glared from the front row at Williams for four minutes before Purana detective Senior Sergeant Stuart Bateson persuaded her to sit down: 'Don't fire them up,' he gently advised.

Mrs Moran then sat and chatted with Purana detectives, who spent years investigating her sons and husband.

Most Purana investigators in court wore their squad tie that included a small Hindu motif. It was a reminder of the ancient Indian proverb from the words of a Purana: 'For the salvation of the good, the destruction of the evil-doers, and for firmly establishing righteousness, I manifest myself from age to age.'

Judy Moran, was dressed head to toe in black – complete with an extraordinary cowboy hat and Darth Vader-style wraparound sunglasses she wisely removed inside the court.

But despite her apparent fashion hints, lynchings have gone out of style.

Judy Moran and Roberta Williams had their habitual pre-court spat where they sniped at each other on issues of etiquette, dead relatives and fashion tastes.

On this day Mrs Williams contrasted Mrs Moran's black look with a white beanie as she had recently shaved her head. Their robust discussions were limited to the court foyer as Mrs Williams was banned from the court after previous outbursts.

She waited outside for the final sentence.

Mrs Moran said repeatedly the death penalty should be returned and Williams executed. She was not such a strong advocate of capital punishment when Jason was accused of the murder of Alphonse Gangitano a few years earlier.

Three former heads of Purana – Inspector Phil Swindells, Superintendent Andy Allen and Inspector Gavan Ryan – were there to see the legal last rites delivered on team Williams.

A film producer and screenwriter slipped in, as did members of the public.

One was quickly reminded that sunglasses perched on top of her head may be acceptable at the races but not in the Supreme Court.

Williams wanted the big finish. He planned to read a prepared statement he had in his blue folder.

When he asked if he could address the court, Justice King firmly said no. 'I expected nothing less of you,' Williams told her. 'You are not a judge. You are only a puppet of the police.'

Williams was taken from the court – his statement unread. He was already yesterday's man. His departing words – 'Aah, get fucked' – do not match Ned Kelly's 'Such is life'.

Superintendent Allen later spoke outside the court, praising his team while pointedly reminding critics who declared police would never smash the code of silence that they were wrong.

The Purana team and the prosecutors went for the traditional court day celebration lunch that looked so unlikely in the dark days of the underworld war.

The wise Justice King, out of her wig and gown and back in civilian clothes, wandered off for lunch. Her work was done. Now she was just Hungry Betty.

# The judgment

*Excerpts from Justice Betty King's sentencing remarks, May 7, 2007.*

'CARL Williams, you have pleaded guilty to three counts of murder and one count of conspiracy to murder. The maximum penalty for each of those offences is life imprisonment.

'These offences occurred during an extraordinary time in the history of this city, in that there was an almost unprecedented level of very public murders of known or suspected criminals. This was ultimately referred to in the media as the "gangland war". The perception of these offences was that there was a distinct war being carried on between rival gangs, firstly, over control of the illegal drug trade, and also on what could be described as a "tit for tat" basis, as reputed members of various gangs were executed in their homes or on the streets of Melbourne. The first of these recognised murders was that of Alphonse Gangitano in January 1998 and they continued on relentlessly with up to 29 persons murdered, although it is apparent that in respect of some of those murders there may have been motives other than gangland warfare. On October 13, 1999, you were shot in the stomach by Jason Moran in a park in Gladstone Park. Mark Moran was present at the time that this occurred, and even upon your own evidence, one of the consequences of this occurring was a high degree of animosity between the Morans and yourself. It is also clear that you and Jason and Mark Moran were competitors in the selling of illegal drugs, which would have done nothing to decrease the animosity that you bore towards each other. I accept that you had a degree of apprehension in respect of the Moran brothers also, which once again is not surprising having been shot by them at close range, and undoubtedly with a warning of some description. I am unable to say whether that shooting and possible warning related to the drug-trafficking business in which you were both competitors, or whether it was a more personal basis. It is unnecessary for me to determine that matter.

You went to hospital and were interviewed by the police as to your knowledge of the person or persons who were responsible for the shooting and you refused to provide any information to the investigating officers. You maintain that was because the Morans had told you that they had a police officer in their pocket, and you did not believe it would be investigated properly. I do not accept that was your reason for refusing to co-operate with police investigators, but rather your reasons related to the supposed code of silence of the criminal milieu in which                              you                              lived.

On November 10, 2000, shotgun damage was observed on the front door of your Hillside home and on a Mercedes Benz parked in the driveway. The prosecutor opened that you believed that the Morans were responsible for such shooting and it is apparent from your evidence that you did blame the Morans for that shooting.

There is no doubt, on the basis of your own evidence, that you were actively looking for Jason Moran so that he could be murdered, you equally did not dispute the role of your adviser in the Jason Moran murder by providing you with information to help locate Jason Moran and assisting you to plan the killing. In the ensuing months various plans were formulated by you and those you had recruited to assist you in the murder.

The driver in the Jason Moran murder and the shooter in the Jason Moran murder were ultimately recruited by you to carry out the murder together.

I heard you give evidence in chief and be cross- examined over a period of some hours. I find that the evidence that you gave, in the main was unbelievable, even incredible at times. It was, in my view, designed to ensure that it would provide no evidence against any person other than those who are already dead, convicted or have pleaded guilty to various offences. You denied any involvement or knowledge of involvement of Mokbel in the murder of Lewis Moran or Michael Marshall.

Not only do I consider you a most unsatisfactory witness, virtually incapable of telling the truth, except for some minor and largely irrelevant portions of your evidence, I find that the manner in which you gave evidence was arrogant, almost supercilious and you left with me with a strong impression that your view of all of these murders was that they were all really justifiable and you were the real victim, having been "forced" to admit at least some of your involvement, by the statements of other members of your group who had co-operated with police.

You do not get to be judge, jury and executioner. These were not vigilante killings, they were matters of expediency to you, these people were either in your way as competitors, or persons that you believed may be vengeful towards you because of other activities you had undertaken, or because of some animosity that you bore towards them.

Your reasons for killing were not justifiable; you acted as though it was your right to have these people killed. That theme constantly came through in the evidence you gave before me.

In terms of the chain of command I find that you were at the top of the chain of command of that gang, and that is entirely consistent with you giving the orders for these people to be killed, whilst not taking an active part in the physical execution of these people. As the counsellor and procurer you were indeed the puppet master deciding and controlling whether people lived or died.

I sentenced you on July 19, 2006, for the murder of Michael

Marshall, after a plea of not guilty and conviction by a jury, to a period of 26 years imprisonment; one year of the sentence you were then serving was made cumulative. Making a total effect of sentence of 27 years, with a non-parole period of 21 years.

Your crimes occurred as I said during a time of what has been referred to as the "gangland" or "underworld" killings. All of those murders, whether charged or uncharged, carry similar hallmarks to these murders. They are invariably executions; a firearm is usually used; they are often in public places such as streets, hotels or places where ordinary citizens would be going about their normal business. Those murders invariably have significant connections with crime or gang-related activity and whilst no ordinary member of the public has been killed or harmed during these killings, those killings have clearly engendered a level of fear within our community as to potential harm of innocent persons, and equally, a concern relating to the degree of lawlessness into which Victoria, as a community, has been plunged. You were responsible to a very large degree for that fear.

There has been intense media coverage of these murders in Melbourne, and whilst you were considered a suspect by many, including the police, the evidence of your involvement was not able to be found, due to the fact that you distanced yourself from these crimes by using others to do the killings and arranging alibis. It was not until the criminal code of silence was broken that those who knew about your involvement began to talk to the police. The sentences imposed on those persons reflect the significant discounts that were given to them for the risks they took by making statements about your involvement.

Whilst you were a suspect and being referred to in the media it was apparent that you were enjoying the game of "being famous". You gave interviews outside court, and appeared prepared to give your views of a variety of matters, and unfortunately the media to a degree pandered to that.

I have a concern that some younger members of the community who are involved in petty crime may be looking to you as some sort of hero. You are not, you are a killer, and a cowardly one who employed others to do the actual killing, whilst you hid behind carefully constructed alibis. You should not be the subject of admiration by any member of our community. You have robbed families of people they love, of sons, brothers and fathers.

I just want to make it clear to all who may look at this sentence that you are not someone to be admired in any way.

I have taken into account the suffering that the families of these victims have endured, as well as the suffering of other innocent people such as Ms Sugars and the owners of the Brunswick Club, also the parents and children attending Auskick, but acknowledge that whatever sentence is imposed, they will probably feel aggrieved as nothing will return their loved ones and no sentence imposed will ever feel sufficient to them.

Your prior convictions are limited in nature and do not relate to any matters of violence. You were convicted in May of 1990 of handling stolen goods, failing to answer bail and possession of stolen property and you were fined a total of $400. In March of 1993 again, at the Magistrates' Court, a charge of criminal damage and throwing a missile for which you were placed on a non-conviction community-based order with conditions of 150 hours of community work, which you breached, but no further action was taken as the order had expired. Finally, in the County Court in December of 1994, attempting to traffic in a drug of dependence, being amphetamine, for which you were ultimately sentenced by the Court of Appeal to twelve months imprisonment with six months suspended for a period of two years. I place no reliance upon the earlier two matters and I place limited reliance upon the latter matter only as indicating that at that stage an involvement in the criminal milieu in which this offence occurred.

Your now ex-wife has three children from previous relationships, a son, aged around 18, and two daughters, approximately 13 and 14. Together with your ex-wife, you have a daughter, called Dhakota, who is aged approximately six, having been born on 10 March, 2001.

Your parents are separated. Your mother has never been in trouble with the law and your father has no convictions. Your father has had significant health problems, particularly in the last few years.

You were educated to Year 11 at Broadmeadows West Technical School and thereafter it was reported that you had a number of short-term labouring jobs. You had a series of labouring jobs, followed by opening a children's wear shop with your wife, which became non-profitable and closed ... You then were working as a semi-professional gambler from that period until being banned from the casino.

You were working as a drug trafficker up to and including the time of the murders.

The circumstances in which you have been held and will in all likelihood continue to be held for a substantial period are of relevance in mitigation of your sentence. You are currently held in the Acacia high security unit at Barwon Prison, which is the maximum security unit of the state penal system. The conditions at Acacia are quite different to those from mainstream prisoners. The visits from family are severely restricted, particularly in terms of contact visits, access out of cells during the day, mixing with other prisoners, and access to phone calls all are severely restricted. This is not what the average sentenced prisoner has to endure by way of conditions of serving a sentence. It is how you have been held, both as a person on remand and as a sentenced prisoner. It is equally evident that this will be the manner of your incarceration for some substantial time.

There are many reasons why persons are in that unit, and in your case, a major part of it is ensuring your safety. You have been in a gang war with other criminals and the issue of revenge being taken by those other persons is not far-fetched. Equally there are many within the prison system that may have a desire to make a name for themselves by causing you harm. Equally those persons who have elected to give evidence against you must be protected from you.

You have also made a statement to the police, which I have had the opportunity to read. You offered to give evidence in respect of that statement but the prosecutor has informed the Court that since you have given evidence in the manner that you have in this case, they would not consider calling you, as they do not consider you a witness of truth.

That concurs with my own observations of your evidence. Accordingly, whilst there is some benefit to you by the provision of the statement, it is of little significance when compared to your criminality.

… You have uttered words of remorse in response to questions asked of you by your counsel but I find that you have no real or genuine remorse for the victims of your crimes, only remorse that you have been caught and lost your liberty.

However, I do intend to impose a minimum term, but that is on the basis of one significant factor only, which are your pleas of guilty to these offences. Whilst I find that you do not have any genuine remorse for the crimes, I am still obliged to take into account in your favour that you have entered pleas of guilty. It is pragmatic and utilitarian to give you a discount for entering those pleas, for by doing so you have prevented this

Court from spending anywhere between five to ten years hearing your trials and the appeals from those trials.

Equally you have released the police officers involved in this task force to move on to other pressing cases that need investigating, and enabled those in the Office of Public Prosecutions to pursue other prosecutions. The amount of money that has been saved as a result is considerable. That behaviour must be encouraged. It must be made clear to all charged with offences, of whatever type, that if they do enter a plea of guilty to the offences that they will receive a real and significant discount. Without your pleas of guilty I would not have imposed a minimum term for these offences, even allowing for the other mitigating material upon which your counsel relied.

Accordingly, I sentence you as follows: on count one, the murder of Jason Moran, you are convicted and sentenced to be imprisoned for life count two, the murder of Mark Mallia, you are convicted and sentenced to be imprisoned for life count three, the murder of Lewis Moran, you are convicted and sentenced to be imprisoned for 25 years.

Count Four, the conspiracy to murder Mario Condello, you are convicted and sentenced to be imprisoned for 25 years.

I further direct that you serve a minimum term of 35 years' imprisonment before becoming eligible for parole. The sentence will commence from this day.

I have already taken into account the fact that you have been in custody since 2004 when determining the appropriate minimum and the sentence and I intend that the new minimum term that I have imposed commences from today. To make it absolutely clear: what I intend is that you are to serve 35 years' imprisonment from today before you could be considered eligible for parole.